A LIFE WITH ANXIETY AND JESUS

FIGHT, FLIGHT ~~OR~~ AND FAITH

NIKKI FLORENCE THOMPSON

Ark House Press
arkhousepress.com

© 2021 Nikki Florence Thompson

All rights reserved. Apart from any fair dealing for the purpose of study, research, criticism, or review, as permitted under the Copyright Act, no part may be reproduced by any process without written permission.

Scripture quotations are from the New Revised Standard Version Bible (NRSVA): Anglicised Edition, copyright © 1989, 1995 the Division of Christian Education of the National Council of the Churches of Christ in the United States of America. Used by permission. All rights reserved.

Fragment of song lyric from Michael Card song 'The Basin and the Towel' reprinted with artist's permission

Some names and identifying details have been changed to protect the privacy of individuals.

Cataloguing in Publication Data:
Title: Fight, Flight Or Faith
ISBN: 978-0-6453220-3-3 (pbk)
Subjects: Mental Health; Christian Living;
Other Authors/Contributors: Thompson, Nikki Florence

Design by initiateagency.com

I loved this book for so many reasons. Nikki has combined her natural gift for storytelling with raw honesty to make for compelling reading. I could not put it down. Like a cool tonic, it reminded me of the treasured and formative years of growing up in our youth group and sitting around bonfires. I was deeply drawn into stories of Nikki and all the people around her, most notably her remarkable late brother. His legacy lives on in his sister, who has provided a treasure for people trying to reconcile their faith and troubles. Despite Nikki's trials, her faith in Jesus only seems to expand and grow.

—Steve Baird, CEO International Justice Mission, Australia

This book is for everyone whose post-2020 life looks like 'a crushed question mark'. In the days of global pandemic and gaping loneliness and loss, Nikki isn't afraid to look hard questions in the eye and offers an answer from the gut of her lifelong and unlikely friendship with anxiety. This book was the soul IV I didn't know I desperately needed.

—Lisa-Jo Baker, bestselling author of *Never Unfriended* and co-host of the *Out of the Ordinary* podcast.

Nikki welcomes us into her story—simultaneously heart-warming and heart-wrenching—of a life filled with anxiety *and* Jesus. Blessedly free of trite theological and pastoral bromides, she invites us to take refuge in the arms of a gracious and compassionate God, one who knows and numbers all our anxious tears.

—Rev Dr Ian Maddock, senior theology
lecturer, Sydney Missionary and Bible College

In writing songs for the church, one of the key questions we ask ourselves is: 'How will the words live beyond the song; how will they go on to travel with the believer through the week?' *Fight, Flight and Faith* is far more than just a riveting memoir. It plants and nurtures seeds of hope in the reader that continue to grow and bear fruit well beyond the final page.

—Rich Thompson, CityAlight

We live in a world where anxiety, grief, and loss have become unwelcome, everyday realities for many people. Amid this chaos, Nikki gives us the gift of her story. Her writing weaves an evocative picture instantly recognisable to anyone who has faced anxiety, walked with grief, or struggled with loss and change. Most importantly, *Fight, Flight and Faith* avoids the trite triumphalism too many faith-centred stories rely on. Instead, readers find solace in knowing we walk the journey together as pilgrims, fully known by a God who is big enough to hold us fast in all of life's storms.

—Sophia Sinclair
Editor, writer, and Australasian Religious
Press Association President 2019–2021.

Reading *Fight, Flight and Faith* feels wonderfully liberating, like starting an important yet difficult conversation we've been meaning to have for a while. Like all great conversationalists, Nikki weaves stories effortlessly, sharing with warmth, honesty, vulnerability, and a seasoning of light-heartedness, so that we too might feel safe in sharing a little of ourselves. There is a disarming and defiant boldness about this work—a willingness to say it as it is, rather than how we think it should be. To explore life's 'in-betweens'— uncertain seasons, unanswered prayers, and unfulfilled longings. To traverse Christian taboos of guilt, shame, and regret. And to suggest that these realities might in fact sit perfectly within a living faith, rather than in opposition to it. We are reminded of the complexity of emotions found within Scripture, not least in the person of Jesus himself. As a Christian brother, I am thankful that this book helps to normalise the interaction between anxiety and trusting in God. And as a pastor, I am thrilled that the church is now equipped with this magnificent resource, as suffering hearts and minds embrace daily dependence on our good and gracious God.

—Greg Cooper
Songwriter & Musician
Gatherings & Music Pastor, St Jude's
Anglican Church Carlton, Melbourne

Fight, Flight and Faith is an honest and gripping account of one woman's journey through grief and anxiety. Nikki's writing is both compelling and heart-warming, her stories rich and vivid. As I read each page, I found myself immersed in every scene, every thought, every emotion. But more than just an enthralling read, *Fight, Flight and Faith* has opened my eyes to the far-reaching impact that anxiety has on those who live with it. I'm deeply thankful for this book and the insight that it will give to many. Truly, Nikki's words are a gift.

—Rhonda Mason, author of *Life Without Cameron*

Nikki Thompson's words and insights are a gift. She clearly and tenderly leads us through a world of anxiety without the false hope of a quick fix. This book helped me better understand my own coping mechanisms and gave me more empathy for the people in my life who have anxiety.

—Devi Abraham, freelance writer and co-host of the podcast *Where Do We Go From Here?*

To Greg
At last, our story.

Contents

Foreword xi
An Introduction Which Is Also a Confession and an Invitation xv
In the Water with God xxv

PART I: THE SHALLOWS

Chapter One: Brewing the Perfection Storm 3
Chapter Two: Safe in the Circle of Campfire Christianity 13
Chapter Three: Before 22
Chapter Four: The Circle Breaks 24
Chapter Five: Trying to be Light 34
Chapter Six: Travelling Heavy 45

PART II: SUBMERGED

Chapter Seven: Anxiety Attacks 57
Chapter Eight: Falling from the Sky in the Year 2000 67
Chapter Nine: In Health and in Sickness 80
Chapter Ten: Secrets 91

PART III: SURFACING

Chapter Eleven: The Wise Woman by the Water 99
Chapter Twelve: Escalators, Aeroplanes, and Stepping-Stone Prayers ... 110
Chapter Thirteen: Anxiety and Its Allies 120
Chapter Fourteen: Running South 133
Chapter Fifteen: Always Winter 147
Chapter Sixteen: Friends Like Penguins 159

PART IV: THE DEEP

Chapter Seventeen: By Christmas 169
Chapter Eighteen: Even on Mountaintops 179
Chapter Nineteen: Seeds of Growth 190
Chapter Twenty: Letting Go of Holy Shoulds 195
Chapter Twenty-One: So Much Bigger 203
Chapter Twenty-Two: Good Surprises 210

Epilogue: Aching Beauty and the Gifts of Anxiety 215
Acknowledgements 219
About the Author 223

Foreword

This memoir is achingly beautiful. It is a rare thing for someone to examine their spiritual and mental health with such care, honesty, and openness. In Nikki's case, this is made possible by her belief that behind all of the sorrow, anxiety, and pain, there is a pair of nail-scarred hands gently holding all things, tenderly bidding us to come and find rest for our souls. A very real hope that threads through this narrative and beyond.

My most formative years were spent with Nikki's older brother. With our being born only a week apart, and with sisters the same age, I felt connected to Greg for brotherhood and wisdom. I recall walking with Greg one afternoon when we were both about nineteen years old, feeling confused about where my life was heading. Casually, I asked him, 'What does God even want from me?' He gently held out hope as he replied, 'To love mercy, act justly and walk humbly with your God.' I have often been reminded since of Bonhoeffer's unique take on community, that Christ on the lips of my brother is stronger than the Christ in my own heart. The brief years I got with Greg are the best example of the truth of this statement.

And Nikki continues in this wisdom stream. *Fight, Flight and Faith* is 'Christ on the lips of my sister' as Nikki presents to us Jesus, not as the one who removes us from life's grief, anxiety, and sorrow, but the one who accompanies us through.

This book is important for many reasons. For me, it brought back memories and emotions that lie just below the surface of my everyday life. Many times, I had to put it down as I quietly wept, recalling the events that Nikki writes so personally and generously about. The loss of Greg was the catalyst, a veritable cannon ball into the calm waters of existence, for a small group of his friends ('The Fellas'). Each of us has been swept away by the ripples to lead lives devoted to proclaiming the good news of an age to come with no more tears or sorrow. This book provided me an opportunity to reflect on the immense gifts that can arise out of tragedy.

But this book is not only a tribute to a brother; it is a deep exploration of the wisdom that can be gained through suffering. One aspect that stands out, and one that will perhaps matter most for many readers, is Nikki's ability to express the nuance involved in looking to Jesus for help with our mental health while also accessing the professional treatment and support that is available to us.

It is no small thing to thread this needle. More commonly, it feels as though we are a pendulum swinging, either too overly reliant on therapy and medication alone, replacing a trust in God's provisional care, or too deceived by the promise of an easily won, victorious Christian life, perhaps believing that God's plan this side of heaven is to remove every valley from our path, leaving us to only experience the mountaintop highs. Ironically, to remove the valleys is actually to lose the possibility of the mountains—and often the appropriate response of faith and worship, too.

To traverse both the valley and the mountain is the gift Nikki gives us all. Her journey of faith is not set at odds with the use of evidence-based treatment when she has needed it. And this perhaps is the greatest insight Nikki provides: seeking professional help is not the opposite of faith.

Several years ago, I had the privilege of playing a new song for the theologian N. T. Wright, a song inspired by my wife and my own experience of losing, in the span of three months, her father to cancer and our own twin babies, born prematurely. The song I shared was based on Psalm 126 and called 'Sowing Tears'. After hearing the song, he said to me with great pastoral care, 'God must love you very much to entrust you with this depth of sorrow.' Even our sorrow is bound up in God's loving-kindness.

The same is true for Nikki. God must love her very much to entrust her with this life story, in all its devastating grief that she so tenderly carries and so generously shares. Through her hard-won insight, we get to grow deeper in our knowledge of God's love. We are invited to walk alongside Nikki as she, like a great guide, points out glimpses of grace and mercy along the road. Those tantalizingly fleeting moments of wonder we might otherwise miss, if not for the careful eye and the gentle voice of one who is walking humbly and hopefully with her God.

To hope is to turn your face into the storm, knowing that the waves don't have the final say. To hope is to reach out for the Father's hand to hold and find that he uses earthly hands to bring help in time of need. To hope is to remain on the dance floor with God until the dance is done.

And this book in your hands is ultimately that. A book of hope.

Nathan Tasker
singer : songwriter : speaker
Co-Director of Art House Nashville

An Introduction Which Is Also a Confession and an Invitation

Straight up, I need to be honest with you. This is not a book about overcoming. Not in the traditional sense, anyway, with no dirt, no doubt, no remnant of groans or traces of tears left at the end. This is more of a 'how are you?' book than a 'how to' book, more of a creased, question-holding companion than a shiny compendium of answers. This story opens with a confession:

My name's Nikki, and I'm an anxious Christian.

Would you believe that it has taken me years to be able to say that confidently—not anxiously—without swallowing, or looking down, or trying frantically to find ways to make it sound less of what it is and more of what I thought it *should* be? And just a heads up, you'll read that word 'should' a lot in here. For such a seemingly simple, innocent word, it actually carries a lot of weight.

I am a believer in the all-loving, ever-present, eternal-living God, revealed to us in Jesus, and I'm also a person who struggles almost daily with the frailty of inhabiting a highly-sensitised body, prone to spikes of adrenaline and hands that tremble, to hyper-vigilance, and vivid, weird and wonderful fears, some of which I'll try to be vulnerable enough to open up for your perusal in this book. Some days just getting out of bed feels hard and heavy.

Of course, it doesn't escape my attention that there's a certain irony in an anxious person writing a book about anxiety, a condition whose very hallmarks are fear and uncertainty and, in my case, more than a liberal sprinkling of perfectionism. Perfectionism, one of anxiety's finest underlings, is like a hungry toddler with a sugar craving, trying to get its sneaky fingers on everything. But it is also (sometimes like a toddler) an excellent interrogator, especially when high on sugar. Who are you, says petulant perfectionism, to speak on a subject you still wrestle with? Shouldn't it be left to the professionals, or at the very least to someone who has successfully dealt with it, once and for all—one who no longer struggles?

Thankfully, compassion and wisdom—oftentimes strong antidotes to perfectionism and soothing balms to anxiety—see it differently. Compassion whispers, slow and steady, that perhaps the best witnesses are not those who are impervious, but those who are still very much in the middle, those who have felt the darkness but also the light, who feel it still, guiding them home even as they stumble. If you are looking for that sort of companion—the second type, the imperfect type, the one who is leaning into light even as she totters—then please stick around and we'll get to know each other more.

I wonder if it would help if I gave a brief history here, something of an upside-down resume, stating my credentials in this field. I am a believer who has experienced anxiety in various forms and manifestations for over twenty years now. I am also a wife, a mother of three, a daughter, a friend, and a writer who dabbles in academia. Anxiety, I have found, strikes indiscriminately, so none of these things say anything about my condition, except that it can be anywhere, in anyone. It does not have one 'type'. I used to suppose anxiety had a particular, feverish sort of passion for introverted, serious, creative types; perhaps those with medium length, infuriatingly wavy brown hair and a weakness for dark chocolate. I've since ridden enough Ubers and shared enough stories (Ubers are great places for writers to collect ideas by the way, that's a free tip) to discover that the big 'A' can affect just about anyone, anywhere, at any time—even burly, tattooed ex-truck drivers, who, it turns out, are very lucid and open about their struggles when behind a ride-share steering wheel. Anxiety just is. My story is unique, and it is universal. It seems that even more of us are suffering than we realise, both outside and inside the church.

In terms of diagnostic terminology, I suffer from *generalised anxiety disorder*, also known by its cute little nickname GAD, which I've always found amusing and appalling simultaneously. GAD, to me, sounds like the name of some sort of garish fluorescent monster, the sort my middle child is obsessively into drawing at the moment. I imagine GAD is bright green and a little flabby, prone to globbing its way about, obscuring one's view of the wider world with its blobby presence, seeping into everything, insidiously. But GAD is not the only diagnosis that inserts its way into this story. There is also the presence of *panic disorder*, PD, marked by panic attacks or PAs (not to be confused with 'personal assistants', unless you want one who trembles and drops cups and is prone to sitting, frozen, in corners). GAD and PD are further joined by a cast of colourful phobias, too numerous to name: phobias of elevators and escalators, of airports and aeroplanes. And then there are all the individual treatments I've tried over the years, like members of so many opposing tribes, who, if they met each other face-to-face, might not be as Zen as they make out. There's cognitive behavioural therapy (CBT) and naturopathy, peppermint tea and pills, aerobic activity and breathing exercises, and years and years of talking therapy.

I've inhaled and exhaled to the count of five. I've taken medication and done meditation.

Now, at this point, some might want to interrupt and interject: 'But wait, slow down. Something isn't adding up here. If you are a Christian, then why are you telling us all this? How can you still be anxious? Doesn't the Bible say, explicitly, *do not be anxious about anything*?'

At which juncture I would want to sip my peppermint tea and quietly reply, 'Yes, it does. I know the verses, believe me. I've read them all. And mulled over them, and worried, and fretted, and searched, and come to this. The fact that anxiety is in the Bible is proof that it exists. Further, it is proof that God understands. Whenever anxiety is the topic of discussion, whether in the Psalms or from the mouth of Jesus himself, I've come to see the focus more as one of encouragement than command. While God wants us to have his peace, he never denies the broken pieces of life this side of heaven. Only in Revelation 21 does he promise to banish tears.'

It is my contention in this book, then, that it is possible to experience anxiety, even in an ongoing way, and still believe. An anxiety disorder is not a faith disorder.

But while my anxiety may be a part of me, and perhaps will be even until I see him face-to-face and he wipes the tears from my eyes, it is not a roadblock to my relationship with God. In fact, I have found it to be the opposite. My experience of suffering with anxiety has drawn me closer under the Father's wing; it has helped my faith to grow. One thing is for sure—God is both bigger than anxiety and big enough to handle anxiety.

But I didn't always see it like this. In between there was lots of breathless running, lots of fighting (between me and me, me and others, me and God, or at least who I thought God was), and questions. You'll read about that here. There were also some slippery, stumbly misconceptions. For many years I thought that to be a Christian I needed to be a light always shining, switched on, bulbs changed, electricity constant. Like an eternally-lit Christmas tree, I thought my best colours always needed to be on display. Until they weren't anymore, or they started to blink, get tired, and die. Until I saw not every season is Christmas.

So this isn't, as I said, a story about overcoming. But it is one about *coming closer* and drawing near. It is a story of *becoming aware* of a widened, expanded faith. Ironically, only when I began to accept my anxiety did I experience healing. It was not my anxiety I needed to vanquish, but my false views of myself and God and that ever-bossy 'should' voice in my head, telling me I should be better, stronger, braver. But… should I? If the God who sent his Son, who wept and sweated blood and died for the world, isn't big enough to love me (and so many others) with my extra-beating heart, my often-churning stomach, and my weird ways, then why did he declare the ultimate death blow to perfectionism and legalism: 'It is finished'?

This, then, is a book for anyone who shares a similar but particularly strong *should* voice in their ear; for anyone who thinks they *ought* to be better. For those in the thick. And for those on the other side. It is even for those looking in. It is, ultimately, a book about healing, but not, perhaps, how or where you'd expect to find it.

A map, a metaphor, and an offering

Before you begin reading, there is one more thing you need to know. The story that follows, while it is told from my perspective, is not mine alone. As you read on, you will come across other words scattered across these pages, fragments of conversations, correspondence, and pieces of poetry, written by my late (and great) brother, Greg van der Kwaak. Or, as he so often signed his name, GVDK.

While this is primarily a book about anxiety, the feeling and experience of a loss of control, it is also a book about loss in other ways. In the end, isn't all loss connected? Can anything truly be separated? For me, this began with the loss of my brother.

When my brother left this world over two decades ago, we lost the solid substance of him: his breath, his goofy all-in smile, the flicker of uncommon understanding in his eyes. But he gave us something too. Greg left behind a treasure trove in the form of his words. Specifically, he left behind a carefully curated and assembled volume of poetry, *The Collected Poems of Gregory David van der Kwaak 1991–1997*.

If grievers are like archaeologists, mining the past for significance, finding wonder and meaning in even the most ordinary objects from their loved one's history, Greg bequeathed us the richest of artefacts. When Greg left his words, he also left behind balm for our cracked and broken hearts. Greg's words spoke for me when I wasn't sure what to say. They simultaneously facilitated and comforted me in my grief and, even more so, perhaps, in the black hole of my anxiety. Ever helpful, my brother gave us continued access to himself and his soul through his pen.

While Greg wrote over one hundred poems, and it isn't possible to feature them all here (though I'd like to), one poem stands out above them all. It is simply called 'atlas'. While I don't claim this poem as belonging to me—it was originally written for someone else—it does have special significance in my life. In seasons of darkness, it is this poem that I have returned to, time and time again, like a flare of guidance in the night.

'atlas' tells of the pain and disorientation of loss, perhaps of a person, most definitely of a sense of strength and security, and of a subsequent search to find a place of peace, a space of rest—what is evocatively described as a 'deep blue lake'. For many years I took this word picture almost literally, constantly on the lookout for still bodies of water, each time hoping I had found 'the one' that would allow me to sit down at last and truly rest.

Only recently do I think that I have come to understand the poem with more clarity. The lake is not a place after all, but an image pointing to something, someone, else. A key clue lies in the epigraph, Matthew 11:28: 'Come to me, all you that are weary and are carrying heavy burdens, and I will give you rest.'

'Come.' An invitation, the gentlest of beckonings. A movement towards, not by force, but by welcome. A promise of embrace. Can there be any sweeter word than this for those who long for relief?

'atlas' has functioned as a sort of map for me over the years (believe me, I am much better with metaphors than actual maps), and the story that follows not only echoes the longing described in the poem, but also takes some of its narrative shape from it too. Perhaps, even in this way, my brother's words continue to guide me.

Over the years, while I've held this poem tightly in white-knuckled fists, I have also felt prompted, on several occasions, to pass it on to others, to people I felt would benefit from hearing its message. And now, here, I want to pass it on to you, too.

I cannot know, dear reader, what you yourself are going through as you read this, but I offer this poem to you before we begin. A gift from me. A gift from my brother.

A gift, perhaps, beyond us both.

atlas* Mathew 11:28

this map has all the important pieces
                              missing,
none of the trails I need to know are
                              marked,
I'm looking for a still alpine lake
        somewhere
                far off—
a lake still enough to sit and stare without fear
and deep enough to understand that
it's all too much to ever understand

come peace, come
rain,
  fall in thick misty sheets
and pass,
leaving me in restful sleep,
head laid on friendly pillow to awake
        tomorrow before my dreamed of lake

it feels as though there's some treasure there
one I'd like to find 'cause my frame can't bear
                              this weight anymore.
I just don't want the years to pass
        my life a wrecked vessel adrift and afar,
it'd just be nice to stand up straight—

FIGHT, FLIGHT AND FAITH

And 'though the space between ourselves sometimes,
Is more than the distance between the stars'
I think that some friends sitting by my lake in
                              the afternoon breeze
might sense something of why this place
is an ease for my cares

The water there is of a blue
        more brilliant than sapphire
and like I said   my lake is deep

For it would take all the aching beauty of a
deep   blue   lake
        to say it all

                              —GVDK

*Atlas—both the Greek god condemned to carry the world on his shoulders as a punishment, as well as meaning a collection of maps.

In the Water with God

I was twenty years old when I discovered that I couldn't get out of the bath.

Technically, my legs still functioned, and my arms had the capacity to hold my body weight, which was at that time not very much. Kilograms, like many other things then, seemed just to be falling off me, disappearing into some unknown place. No more.

Theoretically, there was nothing preventing me from jumping out of that five foot rectangle and running around the house with suds still on my head if I wanted to.

But experientially, in that moment, moving felt like the hardest thing in the world.

I was frozen in fear, stuck solid to the white porcelain bottom like someone had superglued me there. I was a child's hapless toy, lying helpless and stranded, waiting for someone—anyone—big enough and strong enough to rescue me. The warm, sudsy water around me was no higher than my waist, but I may as well have been lost at sea in a tempest, the waves rising to my neck. My hands as they clung to the sides of the bath shook uncontrollably. My heart beat loud and fast, an out-of-control snare drum, my breath caught and snagged on invisible lines high up in my chest. A familiar wave of heat, far hotter than the bath water, surged from my stomach down to my legs and back again.

I was in trouble. And the trouble was both strange and terrifying.

Ironically, I'd taken the bath in the first place as I'd read somewhere that it was relaxing, and I was willing at that time to try just about anything to relax. My muscles were perennially tight, coiled and defensive like a predatory animal waiting to pounce. I hoped that the bath would detangle them. After all, it wasn't even a normal bath, but a fancier one with jets and bubbles. We lived with my grandmother then, and the new build we had moved into together included this particularly shiny, magazine-worthy bathroom. A friend used to come over with the explicit purpose of just 'borrowing the spa'. It was 1999, and something of a novelty. But for me, the bathroom was not the sanctuary it promised to be.

Its position didn't help. The bathroom entrance sat directly across from another room. If I looked out from the bath through the doorway, I couldn't help but see it; the door that was always closed then. The entrance to my brother's bedroom.

In the face of the fury, and my helplessness, I did what I knew best to do. I prayed. For some reason, I don't know why, words from Psalm 61 came to mind. I found myself speaking them out loud to the bathroom. 'Lead me to the rock that is higher than I.' I repeated that one line over and over again to the blank white tiles, above the drone of the jets and the bubbles. Perhaps I hoped, in the act of saying them so many times, I would somehow become lighter, metamorphose and float, bubble-like, above it all. I wanted that peace that passes understanding promised in the Bible so badly it hurt, because the last few years had been beyond understanding.

So I waited and I prayed.

And the words bounced back at me from the tiles.

FIGHT, FLIGHT AND FAITH

The feeling didn't pass. At least not entirely. Not how I wanted it to. But somehow or other, I did make it out of the bath. I did place my slippery, sudsy, uncertain feet on the surface of the floor once more. I did move forward, step by painful step.

Thankfully, that particular incident was isolated. I have never since had an experience of such intensity in a bath again (perhaps also due to the fact that I have been mildly suspicious and averse to baths—to any bodies of hot water promising inflated results—ever since). But those same feelings, the sensation of being trapped in my own body at the whim of my own adrenal system—I have experienced this more times than I can count over the last twenty years.

While I didn't know it yet at the time, my experience in the bath that day had a name. And it turns out, despite what I may have thought then, I wasn't the only one in the world to feel it. There were, I discovered, whole books devoted to it, and diagrams and methodologies. That day in the bath, I experienced a classic panic attack.

Further down in Psalm 61, I see now, years later, what I didn't—or couldn't, perhaps—see at the time: 'For you are my refuge, a strong tower against the enemy. Let me … find refuge under the shelter of your wings.'

Perhaps that's what actually happened. The pain didn't disappear. I didn't float above it. I didn't become some calmer, shinier form of myself. But in praying those words I took shelter under his wings. He still flew, even when I couldn't. And eventually, I made it out of both the bath and the panic.

God was with me in the bath that day, I'm sure of it.

But in the beginning, all I felt was the rising of the waters.

All I wanted was relief.

PART I: THE SHALLOWS

This map has all the important pieces
                              missing,
none of the trails I need to know are
                              marked,
I'm looking for a still alpine lake
      somewhere
             far off—
a lake still enough to sit and stare without fear
and deep enough to understand that
      it's all too much to ever understand

                                        —GVDK

Chapter One

Brewing the Perfection Storm

It might surprise you to hear, after everything I've already told you, that until just before my twenty-first birthday I had barely heard the word anxiety. Not in a medical, pathological sense. Never in relation to myself. As a quiet, people-pleasing child and then as a 'smile, Jesus loves you' slogan-subscribing teenager, the school counsellor's office wasn't even on my mental map. It was just another unknown door, somewhere down a distant corridor, one whose doorknob I assumed I'd never need to touch. Other kids went there; dysfunctional, disobedient kids, the sort with addictions and wayward parents who mistreated them. The type who couldn't keep their spelling lists sorted and their lives on track. I was a good kid from a good home. I made above average grades. I was a member of the Student Representative Council and once, even, School Captain. I quoted these facts at various psychologist's appointments over the years, like rare, luminescent lumps of solid evidence shining in my favour.

'I couldn't have been crazy all along, right?' I'd implore them in my most rational tone, trying to keep my gaze steady and polite, hoping none of the desperation crept through to my eyes. *I used to wear a badge.*

In fact, I'd think quietly to myself, if what happened when I was nineteen hadn't ever happened, if things had gone very differently even after that, maybe I would never have ended up here, sitting on various couches, my present and my past up for scrutiny.

Maybe my name would never have been emblazoned on anxiety disorder's (dis)honour list at all.

Maybe I'd still be okay.

I was trying to do what I'd done all along, the method I'd unconsciously adopted as a child and even tried on for a while as a young adult. I was trying to make everything better by just being good enough.

But it turns out that some things, most things, can't be fixed this way. And that almost everything is much more complicated, more opaque, than it first appears.

***

But before the tide swelled, before the shallows became the waves, before I raised one hand above my head and called for help, for almost the first two decades of my life, the water around me was relatively still. If not entirely tranquil, at least quiet. On the surface my days were bright, suffused with light that filtered through the leaves of the tall green-grey gums that surrounded our suburb like kindly grandfathers, who let us pull at their branches, pick their bark. Atop this surface, in a boat just big enough to fit myself and my tight-knit nest of a family—my mother, my father, and my older brother, Greg—I sailed. If I dared to peek beneath the surface occasionally, into the deep, I sometimes spotted rocks and dark, thorny shapes on the bottom, but I couldn't yet see the things they concealed. The hidden things remained hidden. So long as I had a favourable wind at my back, I kept on sailing.

And the wind was mostly favourable. And warm. And almost always fragrant.

Though I grew up squarely in the northern Sydney suburbs, nature was all around us. An idyllic, upside-down, Down-Under arcadia of golden wattle that sprouted even in winter, where eucalypts mixed with the heady smell of salt that blew over from the sea. Just beyond our gardens the bush grew untouched, wild and vast. We picked cicada shells off tree trunks and stored them, sticky footed, on our clothing. We kept silkworms in shoe boxes and watched giant lizards occasionally appear like unexpected resort guests and sunbake on the tiles around our pool. On midsummer evenings, as my brother and I played cricket with the neighbours on our street, the echo of the tennis ball bouncing around the still-simmering asphalt was overtaken by sounds in the air that buzzed and teemed with life and noise.

This world of wide skies and cicada cries and seemingly endless summers enchanted me. There was a predictability and freedom to our lives then, a simplicity that many look back on now with nostalgia. But there was more, too; another layer that I struggled to articulate, but that I felt, deep within me, as sensitive children often do. Growing up, my brother and I knew that our family was different somehow to other families around us. There was something almost set apart about our parents, something softly mysterious; something beautiful, but achingly tender.

Though we had settled as a family of four (plus one blue Burmese cat) in the middle of 1980s middle-class suburbia, neither of our parents had grown up locally, or even remotely nearby. My mother was the child of Methodist missionaries, born in India where her own mother almost died of acute peritonitis, declared by those nursing her to be the 'most dead alive woman' they had ever seen. With her father up in the hill country, my baby mother was held and tended to by these nurses from her place in a bassinet beside her own mother, who was fighting her post-birthing battle for life. My grandmother, a tough, tenacious woman, slowly and fitfully recovered, until she was just an 'alive, alive woman'; and some years later the family moved to Fiji and finally to the east coast of America, where my grandfather completed his doctorate at Yale. They returned to Australia when my mother was in her late teens, a world of places and people, sorrows, and snatches of joy carried with them.

My mother's early trials did not harden her, but they did perhaps soften her to the extent that she was forever after aware of the difficulties of life, aware and alert for what could go wrong, with a readiness to try and make it better. A gentle, understated, elegant lady, my mum had a way of spreading over everyone around her a warm puddle of light. My friends noticed it too and were drawn to her. Everything she did she poured love into, like she thought it might run out if she stopped pouring it, so she filled it to overflowing. Meals were always large and plentiful, gifts for her kids and loved ones abundant.

My mother had been a social worker working with disadvantaged children before we came along. She had a magic of understanding. Of perception. I remember once standing under the shower, water streaming down my shoulders as I washed my hair, my mum waiting patiently for me outside the cubicle, and having a sudden realisation. My mum always seemed to know what I was thinking, how I was feeling. It was like she could read my mind. But could she? If she could, what exactly did she see?

Her own childhood had been further complicated by a stint in an Australian boarding school prior to relocating to the US. For almost a year, my nine-year-old mother, along with her younger sister, who was then only six, was forced to acclimatise to a long, sterile dormitory room in a country that seemed, to her eyes, strange and foreign. In many ways, from necessity, she also became in this period her younger sister's stand-in mother, when their own mother couldn't be with them. She didn't tell us much from this time, just that once she got her fingers jammed in the door of the communal loungeroom and that the top of her index finger fell off. As if this wasn't horrid enough, the story went on that a fellow student picked it up and, for a moment, thought it was a peanut.

'A peanut!' my brother and I would exclaim and laugh, rolling in hysterics on the floor, pausing only to look at our mother's crookedly reconstructed artefact of a finger, asking her to tell the story again and again. Only years later did I wonder how it must have been for my mother. A child in a boarding school, on her own, with only half a finger. Who held her when she cried, who wrapped her broken finger up for her and looked after her until her own mother could be by her side? Perhaps this is where some of her compassion came from. She knew what it was like to be a child with intense feelings. She knew what it was like to be faced with unexpected collisions with darkness. Perhaps this is why, when we were growing up, she often kept her eyes on the horizon.

My father was older than other parents in the streets and suburbs around us. He had arrived in Wollongong on a boat from Holland in the 1970s and fallen in love with the wide blue skies and endless space. And with my mother. He first saw her across a crowded room at a party of mutual friends, and 'just knew' he was going to marry her. This story, for some reason, always gave me shivers. My father's hair was already lavishly speckled with grey when we were born. He had diabetes and needed to eat well and walk each morning for his health. There were late-night murmurs of potential heart troubles. In moments of vulnerability, my brother and I talked about what would happen if he died earlier than our friends' parents. What then? Though he was almost unfailingly optimistic, moving through life with a mixture of gifting and sheer hard work, we knew he carried things, though we weren't sure what. Heavy things. I saw glimpses of them in his light blue eyes, heard them pressed between the soft tones of his accented English.

I still remember the morning I found the teeth on the bathroom sink; the pink, fleshy replicas bobbing in an ordinary glass of water, abstracted from a mouth. I asked my mother about them first, because she was the one you went to with domestic questions.

'What are those?' I pointed through my parents' ensuite doorway.

Not the sort to ignore her children's questions, my mother paused in her bed making, still holding the dangling piece of sheet she was mid-tucking. 'You need to ask your father about that.' She folded the sheet under, neat and crisp.

My father, routine as a migrational bird, was out on his morning walk. I waited until he returned and showered. By the time I stood before him, the gummy suspects, and all accompanying evidence of them, had disappeared from the bathroom.

'There were some teeth,' I began hesitantly.

'Mine,' he answered. I looked at the impeccably fused members moving the answers in his mouth and tried, without success, to draw a straight line to the glass-jar creature. 'I lost the originals in the Second World War. When I lived in Holland as a child. From malnutrition. Starvation.'

My father's stories about the Second World War came to us over the years, in pieces. One night at dinner in a restaurant, when one of us commented on how quickly my father always finished his meal, never leaving so much as a scrap, he told us about the hunger winter of 1944–45: the last few months before liberation, when the Germans cut off all food supply to their town in an attempt to stop the onslaught of the allies.

FIGHT, FLIGHT AND FAITH

My father's memories both fascinated and horrified me, coming to my young ears in a strange mixture of drama and unreality. In the affluence of the 1980s and 1990s, his stories of his little house in the village, of beds burnt for fuel, of his own father hiding in the ceiling to avoid being captured and taken to German labour camps, and of his seven siblings fighting for a piece of potato, seemed startlingly surreal. But I could see it too, in my mind—my father as a small, skinny boy, curly blond-haired and curious like my brother, standing at the town's soup kitchen, his hands held out like Oliver Twist, 'Please sir, more,' when there was no more.

He later told us he once saw a fellow villager shot dead right in front of him. He rarely spoke of, or even mentioned, the baby sister he lost in this time too. A family absence. An abyss. Some things, perhaps, are too big to begin remembering. His own parents—his kind mama who could make magic with a few pieces of vegetable, and his haunted father who hid in the ceiling—died young, within months of one another. It appeared the years of the war had taken their toll on members of my family even after the liberators had arrived, even after the dancing had begun.

But in the present, we were, or at least appeared to be, a standard suburban family in a four-bedroom house in sunny Sydney. In the present my dad was a successful businessman who put on a suit and tie every morning and took a train into his office in the city. Only occasionally, most often at night, as he sat with his red wine and cheese in front of the television, did I think I might see hints of that other life surfacing, spilling over in my father's tears as he took in the injustices of the world flashing across the nightly news.

My brother and I loved these two gentle souls who had brought us into the world with a faithfulness that mirrored their unbending kindness. We didn't need to be disciplined often, never to my memory with time-outs or groundings. It appeared our parents had a far more effective system in operation, whether they knew it or not. They had our respect and even, in some strange sense, our protection. Neither of us wanted to disappoint them. How much we knew of the struggles of their own early stories back then, stories I have learnt more and more of since and am still learning, and how much we simply intuited, is hard to say. But we understood ultimately that the last thing we wanted to do was hurt them.

It wasn't until I was in my early thirties, and sitting in a cold, sparse psychologist's office in inner-city Melbourne, chewing peppermints to try and calm my nausea, that I learnt of the concept of inherited trauma. Could it be possible that some of my father's early pain, some of my mother's keen sensitivity, even in the smallest of ways, lived somewhere hidden inside me, too?

***

Growing up in 1980s Sydney, lollies were childhood gold. To score a pile of bright, sticky Red Rippers (or Redskins as they were called back then), or white Milkos that would melt into little icicle shapes in the summer sun; to feel the bubble and fizz of Nerds, poured from the packet down a little chute straight into your mouth, was gastronomic heaven. Like any child, I liked sugar, but there was something even sweeter for me, even more addictive: the taste and smell of the approval of others, the syrupy sensation of praise. In my early primary years, this was delivered in the form of scratch and sniff stickers, little bright circles of joy containing words of gushing affirmation: 'You're the best' and 'Keep up the excellent work'.

Unlike lollies, which could be readily bought, stickers were more mysterious in origin. They came in rolls, peeled off one by one from the teacher's desk drawer, which was sometimes locked. But the way to get them in your hands, specifically onto your hand, was crystal clear. The currency for stickers was children's good behaviour and achievement. If you were very good, if you did well, if you excelled, you might just be lucky enough to procure a sticker for your shirt collar or hand. The collar put your accolade on display for all to see, but by far the hand was the best place to store your sticker. To get the full effect, the sticker had to be scratched to let off a sickly-sweet aroma: strawberry, or raspberry, or lemon. I don't know what sort of chemical power they contained to make them smell, but once scratched, the sensation was addictive. Alas, inevitably the sticker would peel off and disappear, and I'd hunger and strive for more.

Once, sometime in lower primary, perhaps inspired by reading of the exploits of the bushrangers, a couple of my friends planned a smelly sticker heist, attempting to steal the entire roll from the teacher's open drawer. I remember standing at the classroom door, feet in both worlds, not wanting to betray or give away my friends, but also not wanting the teacher to catch them, and me. I can't remember if my friends got away with it in the end. It didn't matter. For me, even if they had, I wouldn't have been eager to share the spoils. The stickers, on their own, were meaningless. Worthless. What was needed was the potency of the praise.

Both my parents were intelligent and creative and cherished learning, particularly the world of books, a love they passed onto us. Where my father had been forced to leave school at thirteen and had eventually put himself through university later, becoming an accountant (because when he had looked in the papers on arriving in Australia, that was where all the jobs were), my brother and I had the world of learning laid out before us. Lavish and new. In the small pond of the local primary school, we splashed confidently in the academic waters. My brother excelled at this time in maths and science, with a particular skill of building unique LEGO creations that brought him some acclaim. I loved the warm glow of success when I was praised for a story I'd written or a picture I'd drawn, and along with the item itself I'd carry home the affirmation cupped carefully in my hands, not wanting to drop one piece of it, ready to share and show. I loved the way praise made me feel inside, warm and secure. I learnt quickly that working hard and being good brought measurable results. And the more results I got, the more I wanted. I tried my hardest and did my best, and so long as life went well, the equation was balanced, without any smears or errors.

Stickers were my soft drug in the approval game, a premmie-perfectionist's first foray into the world of people pleasing and competition. Stakes rose over years to include merit certificates, even medals in the final years of primary school. And, of course, later on, marks and degrees.

If I worried too much about making a mistake on my homework, or getting off the school bus too late, or about how the sky looked dark in the distance, like a storm was coming, or worse, a fire, it was put down to my vivid imagination. A tall, skinny kid, not particularly sporty, all my energy was concentrated on the inside. My inner life burnt strong. I feared things, perhaps more than other kids, but I hadn't yet learnt to fear fear.

For many years after my anxiety struck, when various professionals, in a quest to assemble the particular inner puzzle of me, asked me if I was an anxious child, I said no. But that was before I realised that anxiety has a way of lying dormant and even invisible, often for a very long time. Anxiety, like anything else, has its allies, and they aren't always easy to spot. Perhaps the strongest silencer of all in those days, the best ally at keeping anxiety hidden deep at the bottom of my oversized school bag, was my own goodness. I was *good at being good*. I was so good at being good that I fooled even myself.

I didn't know then that good could also have a dark side, a capacity to conceal rather than to heal, and that my goodness, rather than my lack of, would ultimately lead me into trouble. I was unwittingly brewing a perfection storm.

Chapter Two

Safe in the Circle of Campfire Christianity

Some people have dramatic conversion stories, complete with audible voices and spine-tingling moments of epiphany. Others stumble into faith reluctantly after years of resistance, seeing the light only at the end. The opening lines of my own Jesus story fit neither of these models.

My faith arrived gently on the breeze of my thirteenth year, full of tender warmth and light, with the smell of wood smoke and the strum of steel-stringed acoustic guitars under a star-canopied sky. My faith was forged around these campfires, shoulder to shoulder with friends. Together we leaned towards the flames and felt ourselves glow. Darkness still existed, but it lived only in the distance then, beyond the circle, in the spaces between the shadows of the trees.

In the beginning, I was full of hope and trust, and if the darkness ever crept inside me, which it sometimes did, I only needed to step closer to the fire and it melted away. And we too were bearers of the light, ready to take the embers to the world in our outstretched hands, not yet fearing being burnt.

***

Before I started following Jesus, I followed someone else. From the moment I could walk (maybe even before), I travelled in the silver-threaded slipstream of my older brother, Greg. Greg did everything that little bit before me, and like so many younger siblings, I watched his movements with avid curiosity and concentration. It helped that he had a natural, understated knack for leadership, a sensitive surety, and an intellectual bent to enquiry that made him eager and open to exploring the world, which in turn opened the world up to me. My brother, more than anyone else, showed me how to live in the spaces outside our front door.

When I was around nine years old my world shifted suddenly as my brother left the cosy enclave of our small, on-the-edge-of-the-bush public school to attend an all-boys private middle school a bus and a train ride away. Every morning I watched as he rose early, dressed in a blazer and tie, and heaved a bag worthy of a week-long hike on his shoulders as he left the house. I, for one, was not convinced of the value in this new endeavour. The level of effort involved seemed to outweigh the benefits. Plus, I missed him. He was my compass point. In almost every childhood photo of the two of us, my head is turned to the side and tilted upwards, looking not at the camera, but at my brother. I took almost all my cues from him. This time he had truly gone ahead. But it was here, among the hyper-masculine jostling of boys on the awkward cusp of manhood, that Greg met a tall, gentle giant of a boy called Scott. Scott was good at rugby and could eat not one, but two McDonald's hamburgers in a single sitting. One day, perhaps over hamburgers, Scott invited Greg to the youth group at his church, and for a reason unknown to me, Greg accepted the invitation. This single interchange set off a chain of events that would affect not just our Sunday mornings, but our lives.

The youth group was called Teens Club (or TC, as we soon learnt to call it for short). We discovered early on that church organisations are packed full of catchy, slightly cringy acronyms for those in the know. Greg went along on Sunday morning and returned again the next week, reporting that the leader remembered his name. I was equal parts fascinated and suspicious of this new venture. Along with my parents, I wondered what this place was that had captured so much of Greg's energy. Was this just a new fad like Greg's early obsession with LEGO? Would he grow out of it?

Greg's church life had an intensity beyond the tea-drinking, biscuit-dipping Sunday ceremony I had experienced when I visited Sunday school with my best friend, Emma. I wasn't sure how I felt as I watched my elder brother dive in headfirst. It wasn't until he showed me what it looked like close up, from within our own story, that I started to really see it. And finally, to live it, for myself.

***

It was mid-1990, winter, and I recall a long, winding drive from Sydney to the New South Wales Snowy Mountains. We stopped down the South Coast at Nowra, to pick up Greg from the affectionately termed 'Tree stump' campsite, where he'd just finished up one of his first youth group camps. I didn't know then how much that out of the way place, that small, seemingly ordinary patch of tall green trees and rich dirt, sloping down to a river, where cows grazed and you had to tread carefully so as not to step in something, with its songs, smells, warmth, and simplicity, would become so extraordinarily central in my late childhood to early adulthood.

Perhaps I caught a whiff of it on the wind, or in the winsome freedom in my brother's eyes as he climbed into our car and we carried on driving into the next week of our family snow holiday. A holiday, like a small collection of others across the next few years, that I didn't know then would become so significant to me in later times.

We stopped to try on boots and skis—an amateur set of hopefuls trying on a new skill lightly, with a wistful elation—and I remember the following days of laughter and discovery, flying down slopes with my father who failed to see the signs saying to go no further, with Greg negotiating the slopes solo in his singularly independent and competent way, and my mum doing what I would most likely do now were I to go with my own kids, sipping tea and reading in the coffee shop, welcoming us back proudly from our adventures with steaming mugs of hot chocolate.

That is the delicate background to those precious days. But in the foreground is the prominent circle of memory I cannot seem to escape—nor do I want to—where I see a set of bunk beds in a holiday rental at the foot of the mountains, and a blond teen-man, self-conscious about his acne, always trying to flatten the curl from his hair, leaning over the top bunk—leaning down to his kid sister beneath—with a singular question that pierced the crisp night air and punctuated the tempo of our early days with an emphasis that rings and resounds even now:

'Hey, Nik?'

'Yeah.'

'I've been thinking… how can I love you more? I want to know how to love you better. Like Jesus.'

If I were a fish and my brother a fisherman (and didn't Jesus say…), that was the first time I clearly remember the line dropping and bobbing lightly before me, and my wanting to bite. Love came to me in action as a question—in particularity. My brother wasn't just professing the Christian creed to love others as himself; he was striving to make it happen. The universal command became personal in a small, borrowed bedroom somewhere in Jindabyne in the 1990s. That was the first real time I saw the love of the Father as he reached down to me through the faithful voice of my brother. And I followed.

***

Teens Club was led by a large man called Ken, arrived in Australia via the deserts of Arizona, who rarely wore shoes. Ken had a loud, husky, unapologetic voice and a serious chewing-gum habit. With his radical ideas and his ability to throw himself full-bodily into whatever the kids were doing, parents *within* the church had reservations about his personality and unconventional way of doing things, let alone those from without. But, to his credit, Ken held steadfast to his belief that teens were capable of more understanding and commitment than was commonly assumed. They didn't need the gospel news watered down for them or served as a sugary side dish alongside the main dish of games and fun. Although there were many fun times, many games, God and his word always came first. If it really were the truth, Ken reasoned, kids would sit up and pay attention.

I remember the early months of listening to talk about Jesus, at once wonderstruck and, if I'm honest, weirded out. On one of my first weekends away with church, I sat cross legged on the floor in a cabin discussion group while a curly-haired leader called Mel talked about how she longed for heaven. I observed how she reflected, without a hint of irony, on the fact that this world was passing away, groaning sick for another one. I can still feel the shock in my own young heart and mind. It sounded so surreal, so mystical, so literally beyond this world. Were these people for real? Or were they all trapped in some sort of fairytale land, and should I just skip back down the path and disappear into the woods again, back to the real world, before it was too late?

But one weekend, while singing around a campfire, I felt the solid assurance of it seeping deep inside me, bones to marrow, that this indeed was the truth. Jesus had died for me, and I wanted to live for him. I gave my life over to the one who gave his life to me. I don't remember the exact details, what I said or who I told first after I said it, if my words to God, my prayer, was profound or clumsy; but I do remember the shift that took place. What before had seemed literally un-believable was now truth. And life.

I didn't run away into the woods; I stayed squarely in the centre, until everything else radiated out from there. I fell in love with Jesus, and without realising it, I also entered into an intensely devoted relationship with 1990s Christian culture.

***

I guess you could argue that I was 'good' at being a Christian teenager. Learning about God suited me. I loved all the opportunities to read and discuss ideas: weekly Bible studies, prayer groups, Sunday meetings. I took notes and leaned in close, not wanting to miss a detail. My introverted, sensitive soul loved the contemplative side of my new faith too; chances to sit quietly in thought and in prayer, often with a notebook in my hand, in nature. These times were always shorter than I would have liked. It turns out not too many teenagers had the same affection I did for thought and silence. At home, I lay on the floor of my messy bedroom, books and clothes strewn all around me, passionately singing along to Keith Green songs, or Jars of Clay, ascribing personal significance to the lyrics. My shy, awkward teen persona, never entirely comfortable in the complex new social world of co-ed high school where my bad skin and new hormones made me feel more freak than fit-in, found refuge at church, where things like what you looked like didn't matter—at least, not in theory, not entirely, not if you didn't let them.

Like many of my church friends, I was earnest. I wanted to share my faith with my school friends who were floating helplessly out in the world, lost and decidedly 'non-Christian'. This part, however, didn't come so easily to me. I was, no doubt, clumsily self-righteous, putting my Dr Martin booted foot in my own well-intentioned mouth as I attempted to go out and make disciples. I remember sitting outside on a bench at school one lunchbreak, beneath the trees, the sounds of the schoolyard loud and chaotic around us, looking into the pained eyes of one my closest school friends. While I was decidedly a good girl, I gravitated to those on the fringe, perhaps to those whose emotional sensitivity matched mine, even if our lifestyles were dramatically different. I had my mother's listening ear, and as my friend spoke, I did not move my eyes from her face. I listened as she shared the latest instalment of her loaded story of heartache, of separated parents with complicated histories, of her own fraught relationships with boys, of darkness and depression. I clumsily tried to speak 'two ways to live' over her, as I'd been taught, praying fervently inside that she'd be open to Jesus, to coming to church. I could almost see her there. If I could just draw her in, I told myself, she'd be okay, all her problems would become, if not non-existent, at least a lot better. Didn't—hadn't—mine?

I believed in God. I perhaps believed a little too much in every little extra piece of what I was taught and also those who taught me, probably more than they intended. I worshipped my attractive, funny, mostly still-very-young-themselves youth group leaders in a degree close to idolism.

But in the same way that I believed too much in things I shouldn't have, in another way I didn't perhaps believe enough. I subscribed wholeheartedly to the idea of amazing grace, to God's unmerited gift of salvation borne out of his deep love for us, in theory, and I was always quick in words, verses, letters, and hugs to reassure my friends if they ever doubted; but for myself, I struggled. I was both committed Christian and strung-out high school perfectionist, still the child longing to please. Sometimes these identities got muddled. To be a good Christian, my nagging inner voice told me, I had to be a good student, good daughter, good friend. Good. Good. Good. It's not surprising that I got tired a lot in my later school years.

Perhaps the most defining moments for me at this stage of my life were the youth group camps I would attend every school holiday, whether in the bush in winter, or the beach in summer. These were my escape. My breath of fresh air.

At camps, I felt I belonged like no other place I had ever experienced, except my own home. We often talked in those days, amongst ourselves, about these times away from it all being like 'a taste of heaven', with a whole bunch of young believers living together, serving one another, learning alongside one another. We were taught to love each other, and there were few places in the world I loved more than the various camp cabins I shared with my fellow believing friends. With these girls I felt I could share almost anything, and in the teen years, when you often feel like you are an inexperienced, ill-equipped circus performer walking a trapeze, at any moment prone to falling through space, they were my soft place to land. My brother's friendship group grew too, no longer just Scott, but a solid group with their own identity and even a name as time went on: the Fellas.

Each night on camp, after the Bible study and physical exertion of the day, we'd line up for our hot chocolates and raisin bread from the camp kitchen and, rugged up in our Ugg boots and on-trend 1990s check flannel shirts, make our way down to the circle of logs beyond the cabins. Here the air smelled of wood smoke, and the leaders urged the flames higher and higher, until they nearly touched the leaves of the trees above, but somehow never did. We'd take our seat in the circle, and we'd share and pray and sing.

There's a hushed peace in my mind as I remember it, even now.

In another psychologist's office years later, when I was asked to share a place I felt totally secure, this is the place I returned to. This circle.

I never felt safer than then, I said. Never again.

But the memory itself, perhaps like all memories to some extent, holds within it elements of nostalgia, even mythology. I longed to go back to a time when things were better, brighter, clearer, and much, much easier. But I also wanted to return to a time where I hadn't yet met real struggle in my faith. If I felt secure, perhaps it was a sense of God's arms around me, but perhaps it was also, at least in part, the result of the cosy world I had built up over the years around God.

When that security was stripped away, when pain came inside the circle as it surely later did, I had to rediscover what it meant to rest in God, whether under the stars surrounded by friends or in my own bed. Alone. I had to learn a new expansiveness that was much bigger and wider and higher than any flames.

I do not mean to say my faith then was not real. I believe with all my heart that it was. But it was also just the beginning. In the beginning my faith was a pure, secure space. Genuine, but tender. Grounded, but on untrodden ground. True, but untested. Encircling, but also enclosed. In the beginning my faith was safe. But, in many ways I didn't yet realise, it was also very, very small.

Chapter Three

Before

I still remember the order of *Before*. Before the news at the door. Before the unalterable. Before anxiety burst in uninvited with its disruptions and demands, spreading its dis-order.

In the land of Before, I finished high school and postponed university and planned a solo trip to Holland, my father's homeland, barely faltering as I stepped over the threshold and onto the aeroplane, carrying anticipation and hope full in my bag.

In the land of Before, I didn't need to check the plane's exit signs repeatedly or tremble at the first sign of turbulence. I didn't fear breaking into the captain's cabin to tell him that he needed to turn around and take me home. NOW. (To be clear I never actually did this, but I did think of it, often, in times to come.)

In the land of Before, when I found myself in a Dutch hospital with a mysterious stomach-ache (that turned out to be bad food poisoning from a bad ice cream at a kitsch tourist site), despite the doubled-over pain, and the bedpans, and the scurrying around of official-looking doctors speaking a foreign language, I didn't worry I was dying from some catastrophic disease.

FIGHT, FLIGHT AND FAITH

When I got out, I'm pretty sure I didn't think twice before I ate an ice cream again.

In the land of Before, my future unfurled like a ribbon, twisting with colourful choices, and though I didn't yet know all the answers, I did not fear the unravelling.

In the land of Before, my muscles were still loose and my heartbeat even. My blood did not burn, nor my stomach always coil. My neck was not always tight.

In the land of Before, I did not have my hands perpetually to my face, like Munch's *Scream*. I wasn't ever vigilant, a vigilante always patrolling for threat, thinking it all lay in my hands.

In the land of Before, I did not question every time a loved one left the house, even for a loaf of bread or a bottle of milk. I did not feel the urge to cling to them by a thread, to try to keep the fabric of the future from tearing.

In the land of Before, I did not always ask 'what if' but could usually see 'what is'.

In the land of Before, I did not need to think about my breathing, whether it was deep or shallow or where exactly it was coming from. I did not fear the sudden loss of it.

In the land of Before, if I was sometimes scared, I was not immobilised, and I knew how to worry without losing myself inside my own mind.

In the land of Before, fear was explainable, and mostly surmountable, and resolutions could turn into solutions.

In the land of Before, life may have been uncertain, but it was not perilous. And I still trusted enough to take some chances.

In the land of Before, I could still fly without feeling like I was falling.

For the longest time, when After arrived, all I wanted was to return to Before.

I believed the loss of it was the biggest problem of all.

Chapter Four
The Circle Breaks

That Wednesday began insignificantly. There was no drum roll, no ominous overture leading to a crescendo. No voice from the sky told us to lean forward and get ready for what was coming. For the first twelve hours we walked about in our usual skins, carried along with us our everyday, low tide, bobbing emotions.

I went to work at my parents' business in the city, dressed in heels and business attire, playing casual grown-up while earning some money with my friends in the final weeks of the summer holidays before I started university. I caught a bus to pick up a box from Sydney airport, the excess of my recent travels in Europe and Canada, the spoils that hadn't fit into my bulging suitcase. I met an old friend for lunch in a city park. We talked about bicycles as we sat on the lawn and watched the lycra-clad midday fitness fanatics ride by. We talked too long and loose, and I lost track of time. I ran to jump on another bus, cutting across a busy city street recklessly, just to make it back to work on time. I was still at least eight hours away from being acutely aware of my every movement.

It was hot. It was late February. I can't remember if it rained that day. It did after. For a full straight week the clouds spilled out and over, as if the sky were undertaking rituals we didn't yet know how to do. That, unlike almost anything else that followed, seemed to make sense. I must have eaten something for dinner. I changed from my dark, heavy work clothes to go out to Bible study. I wore a pair of baggy shorts and borrowed an oversized white T-shirt from my brother's wardrobe. Though I never wore that shirt again, for years afterwards I couldn't bring myself to throw it out.

My friend Katelyn picked me up, and we drove to Claire's house where our group was meeting. I'd always liked Claire's place. She had fairy lights in her room, which made it ultra-cosy, especially at night, and everything was always neater there than in my own. The Bible study began. Emma, Katelyn, and I sat together, and we worked on the questions on the sheet handed to us by our leaders, Matt and Karen. I remember where we sat, in a little alcove off the main lounge room. I remember that we weren't taking it that seriously. We were laughing loud, and a little crazy, as only young friends with no responsibility and too much time and air can.

And then the phone rang. There were footsteps. And after that, everything changed.

***

Across the busy room, through the chaos and chatter, Matt stood, straight and still, looking over in our direction. I'm not sure if others felt it too, or if it was just me, but it seemed like someone was dimming all the lights, turning down all the sound. The words wove their way towards me. Distant. Faint. But somehow still very clear. *I need to talk to you, Nikki.*

Matt and I stood on Claire's front porch, dark, with no fairy lights, and faced one another, and he somehow said the words. I can only imagine now, years later, how difficult they must have been to form, how his throat must have clamped to hold them in, how each syllable must have scraped and tunnelled its way out. *There's been a car accident. Greg. A tree. Dead.*

'You're joking.' That's all I remember saying back. I felt my eyebrows rise like they were being manipulated. Like I was a toy puppet, nothing more than wood and wire, and someone else was pulling the strings of my reality.

We went back inside, briefly. There was some insignificant discussion about my bag. My limbs must have ceased working, because Emma and Katelyn said they'd take care of it. With an arm to my shoulders, Matt guided me to the car.

We drove home silently, through humid, moonlit streets where tall gums danced spectral in the summer breeze. I leant away from Matt, hunched towards the door, my forehead pressed into the cool surface of the glass. *This is it*, I said to myself. To the trees. To the dark expanse of clouded-over sky. *I need to figure out how I will cope, so that when I get home I'll be prepared, so that I won't fall apart.* I was naive, I was grief-green. I didn't yet know there was no preparing. That there was no such thing as not falling apart. I think I prayed. I'm not sure. I know that I was thankful to have heard the news from someone else, and to have a moment to let it sink in, even if only to the very surface of my skin, before facing my parents.

Matt offered to come to the door with me, but I refused. Why did I refuse? I don't know. Was it because I already knew, beyond consciously, that what awaited was too tender to be exposed beyond the family eyes? Was I like a buffer, already closing in, wanting to protect those I loved?

My parents met me at the door. Two trembling teardrops. One of the things I have always loved about my father is his posture. Though he is tall, he does not stoop. 'An upright Dutchman,' my mother-in-law, Roz, now says of him. A straight-spined chiropractor's dream. That night, when he answered the door to me, my father was bent, doubled over, crumpled. A crushed question mark, no answer in sight. Like a tree pulled from the soil in an unforeseen storm, I felt the groan of his sudden rootlessness in the bend of his back, as the weight of the world fell upon him. Upon my mother. Upon us all.

And with everything in me, with every last ounce of muscle, every fibre of strength, I braced.

***

It took me less than twenty-four hours to learn that grief's floundering love language is flowers and casseroles, and that grievers, those who lose, must also become those who receive. While my parents went off on the loneliest of journeys, to identify my brother's body in a country police station several hours away, I stayed home hunting for vases and making room in the fridge. I spent the day answering the door to beautiful bouquets and broken faces, to friends and family gripping ribbon-bound offerings, trying to keep their own loose pieces bound momentarily secure to care for us. I tried, in turn, to stay tied up enough for them.

That day, and those following, are now marked in my memory with that strange grief mixture of indistinct and unforgettable. I remember only two phone calls from that morning. The first, a friend of Greg's who was outside the immediate church network. When I answered, she spoke in the normal voice, not the grief voice, and instantly I knew she didn't know. And in the not knowing she was still a thousand lightyears away.

'Hi, can I speak to Greg?'

Long pause. 'I'm sorry, he isn't here.'

I remember apologising, fumbling around for the right number of words to cushion the moment when I needed to come out and say it. 'I guess you haven't heard yet.' And then I said the rest.

She responded not in words but in sound. There was a wail, long and high, like a wild animal screaming down the receiver at me. I felt like I was standing in a clearing and the sound alone was chasing me.

The second phone call I initiated. We each had our lists, hastily drawn up, Mum and Dad and I, of who we had to inform. I dread to think how they did theirs. Top of my list was my grandma, who was away on a trip with her sister that weekend. When I reached them at last, I was relieved to find it was Margaret who answered the phone first.

Her voice was holiday happy, light, buoyant as an air balloon. 'Hi, Nikki, how are you?'

'I'm okay, no, actually, um, I'm not really.'

I tried to do the preface, so awkward, so fumbling, apologetic once more, as if it were my fault that I was calling. This time, I wanted to seal off my ears from the sound my puncture wound was about to make.

'Are you sitting down?' I asked. That's what you say, right? Maybe I thought the shorthand itself would do the job for me, of coming out and saying it. 'There was an accident.'

Staccato beat.

'Greg.'

Inhale.

'No, not a joke.'

Margaret offered to be the one to tell Grandma. She was like that, tough and kind. I accepted.

Two people offered to drive my parents on their darkest of road trips. Emma's father, John, and also my mother's brother, David. Because he was part of the family, insistent, and younger, I suppose, Uncle David was given the role. They needed to head down south towards the coast, a beautiful scenic drive in normal circumstances, to the town of Braidwood, near where Greg and his friend had been camping that weekend. It had been a last-minute trip to cheer his friend up after a recent relationship breakdown. Not unusual; at least, not initially. Greg did these sorts of things all the time, going out of his way for a friend. He loved the outdoors.

I never asked what my parents talked about on the way down, if they stopped for a drink or a toilet break. I'm not sure if any of them would have been able to tell me anything clearly, anyway, had I asked. They were on shock time, in shock space. Compelled forward by beyond-believable reasoning.

The day passed, and I was glad for something to do. I dug my hands further into the refrigerator, lifting pasta bakes, creating space for a giant fruit platter from one of Greg's friends. I cut stems of white lilies, and when we ran out of glass containers, I asked my friends to bring me more.

My parents and uncle arrived back at last from their six-hour round trip. Strangely, I don't remember too much of their re-entrance into the house from that other place. Perhaps I have blanked it out. What I do remember is my uncle. He was younger than my mum by considerable years. The baby of her family. He was dark haired, strong jawed, and good looking, prone to easy laughter and comfortable joking. He walked straight through the hallway and to the kitchen table, taking the seat closest to the window. And then he bowed forward, his head in his hands. He wept. I went over and embraced him as he sat, all my nineteen years of awkwardness forgotten in the force of the moment.

I recall only snatches of my parents' words. How Greg looked. How it was him, but how it wasn't, too. Some things shouldn't have to be seen. I'll leave it at that. Suffice to say, I have lived in a hushed sort of awe of my parents ever since that moment they looked the bitter reality of death square in the face of their own son.

And ever after, I have made it my mission to never break them like that, or in any way, ever again.

***

My memories of the funeral are oddly selective. I remember the outfit I wore, a long floral Laura Ashley dress, but not how I wore my hair. I recall waiting at the window, watching for the arrival of the funeral cars, but not the trip to the church. I can picture walking down the aisle to the sad stares of so many eyes, but not who led our strange anti-processional. Bizarrely, I would walk down the very same aisle five years later for my wedding, to beautiful acoustic music and hundreds of smiles, many of them the same faces that at the funeral were drawn heavy with grief, frozen with incomprehension.

My father spoke the longest eulogy, in English first, and then in Dutch, the guttural sounds so melancholy, so noble, as he sought to translate the flow of his love for his son, impossible in any tongue, for his relatives overseas. One aunt and one uncle had made the journey to represent the Dutch family. There had been a last-minute scramble for passports, favours called in somewhere for special expedition under the circumstances. I had caught my dear uncle practising his English words on notecards the night before in Dad's small study, intended for delivery to my mother and I. Phrases like *I am so sorry for your loss*. And *we love you very much.*

My own speech was typed out, two short pages to sum up a lifetime of knowing and being known. Emma sat in one of the front pews nearby, poised to read it if I could not. But I didn't need to pass the baton; somehow my voice held out, only breaking at the end when I attempted my final words. People read poetry and shared memories, and Nathan Tasker sang 'When I survey'. At the end of it all, the Fellas carried the casket out on their shoulders. There was an Arthurian sort of nobility to this that Greg would have liked. One of them was too overcome with emotion to do it. Sometimes the weight of love is so heavy, it's too much to bear.

But somehow, I bore it, only snapping once. As we followed the coffin out to the courtyard, a small, older woman stepped out into the passageway and stopped me. 'Do you remember me?' She looked up at me as she held onto my wrist tightly. 'I knew you when you were little,' she continued, her eyes asking me to reply. But I didn't remember. Nor did I want to. Not then. It was not the time for long-lost reunions. I pulled her clasping hand from my wrist, pushed her away a little too roughly and walked forwards. Grief can be a wild thing when it's let loose. The shock and awe of grief sent my friend Tori running from the church, midway through the service, to vomit in the bathroom. But I did not run. I did not gag. Not yet. For the most part, I kept my own responses tame, corralled, neat as my stockings tucked into my high-heeled shoes.

There was another set of unfamiliar faces wanting to talk to us that I did not treat so resentfully. Rather than the forwardness of the older lady, the two men who approached the funeral car as we were ready to drive away to the crematorium were hesitant, almost apologetic. They singled out my father to direct their words. 'We are from the university,' they said. 'We taught your son. He was a wonderful young man. A wonderful student. Full of so much promise.' My father leant forward and shook each of their hands. And I even managed a smile. Their words were far more valuable than any bunch of flowers.

Ken warned us ahead about the crematorium, about the coldness, and the curtain, and about the moment of vanishing that would come at the end, like a cruel magic trick. So we were prepared and unprepared. Perhaps the magic act worked; I remember very little. A select group of us broke off from the larger funeral gatherers and drove the short distance to the memorial gardens. But where the funeral had been more like a thanksgiving service, full of music, and poetry, and personal words laced with detail and particularity, the crematorium was like a foreign ceremony that we watched from outside. At the funeral, I was able to think of heaven. No matter how much it hurt to say goodbye, I knew Greg was somewhere far more beautiful than we could imagine. At the crematorium, it was all about death.

We returned again to the church for the post-service afternoon tea, where people were waiting for us once more as we stepped out of the mourning vehicles. I hadn't realised running a funeral was so much like throwing a party, where everyone wants to talk to the hosts. I can't remember much of what happened that afternoon, the details of who exactly I talked to, or who talked to my parents, or how many times I went to the bathroom or stretched out my hands to receive a card, a kiss, or more flowers. I know there was a large spread of sandwiches and, in normal times, what would be a mouth-watering array of cakes and slices. I remember thinking passingly that they seemed out of place, too heavy and ornate, with their layers of icing and cream, like kids who had got the wrong memo for dress-up day at school. I remember also wondering who would take them all home at the end, when they'd hardly been touched. I remember the Fellas' arms around me and how much simple touch conveyed when words weren't enough. And I remember, also, the multiple compliments I received. About myself. About Greg. The ones about my brother I was more than happy to hear. I was his head cheerleader, after all. I raised my pompom willingly to every single one. They could have told me, right then and there, that he was a saint, and I would have agreed. But the ones about myself, these I wasn't so sure about.

FIGHT, FLIGHT AND FAITH

'You are doing so well,' people said. 'You are being so strong. What a great witness you are. Your faith, your peace, is on display so clearly,' hushed tones confided. 'Your brother would be so proud of you.' I know they meant well, intending each and every one for good. For blessing. Not for burden.

But I just wasn't sure how to respond. The compliments both warmed me and confused me. Gave me solace and filled me with unease. Deep inside myself, in a cavern-like place I had barely allowed the shock and grief to seep into yet, they made me ask a silent question: What would they say if I wasn't strong, if I had fallen apart? Would that mean I was a disappointment to my brother? To God?

It seemed, at least to my mind then, that there were only two choices on offer: to cope, or to not. To give thanks, or to despair. To trust, or to weaken. All early evidence seemed to be leaning in one direction over the other, so I followed. I chose strong.

S-T-R-O-N-G.

And for the next few months, I did everything I could to keep on spelling it out, in the clearest, most convincing voice I could.

Chapter Five
Trying to be Light

Two weeks after my brother's funeral, I started university for the very first time in the same place he had only recently left, expecting to return, for the last time.

Reading this now, perhaps you are thinking what I am thinking so many years later. Why did I return to 'normal life' so soon? Didn't anyone try to stop me, tell me something blandly gentle and chicken-soup clichéd like, 'There's no need to rush, to push, there is plenty of time'? Perhaps they did. I can't remember. What I can remember is how radioactive I felt. Anytime anyone who knew me came near, I could almost see them startle, tense, take a step backward from the toxic new territory of my grief. They wanted to help, but perhaps, if even a little, they were scared of being infected or of saying something that would only make it worse. At the time, in grief time, in still-very-much-in-shock time, my decision to barrel headlong back into life seemed no less crazy than anything else. I didn't need more silent hours in suspension. I needed to keep going. I needed to move forward. I needed, if I'm honest, to get out of the house. Out of my own head. I wanted to plant my feet firmly on earth that didn't tremble day and night with aftershocks. To feed off the energy of people unlike me, who didn't walk around enclosed in invisible, automatic, signal-sending forcefields. Perhaps I just wanted a break.

So it was, fourteen days after the landscape of my known world seismically shifted, I found myself studying the inscrutable fine print of timetables and room numbers, navigating mazes of corridors, and mouthing polite greetings to strangers who sat beside me with notebooks and pens poised to write their new-stage-of-life stories. Just a fortnight after I formally farewelled my brother from the front of my church, I sat at the back of crowded lecture theatres, listening to opening remarks on my various courses—English literature, sociology, linguistics, and anthropology—all distinct disciplines, all with different emphases, but with one overarching, hard-to-miss message. *Welcome to your new life of learning,* they proclaimed confidently. *Your journey begins here. The world is now as big as you make it. The opportunities are yours for the taking.* Nowhere, not even in the fine print, did I see anything written on what would happen if they were taken from you.

It seemed there was an orientation procedure or course for almost everything at university, from clubs, to sports, to how to footnote your sources correctly (because, let's be honest, who ever really knows how to do that?), to how to use the computer labs. But never did I see a sign with an arrow or a sign-up sheet that read 'Grief 101: How to cope at university immediately after loss'. Nowhere, not even in the ten-storey-high black monolithic structure of Fisher Library—the ugliest building by far at the University of Sydney (USYD)—crammed full of books with yellow, curling-at-the-corners pages and strange-looking librarians who appeared hardly ever to venture beyond its electronic doors, was there an answer for the 'how' of my particular story.

How did a nineteen-year-old girl whose brother had only just died walk into a world of new when she hadn't yet processed the old? How did she skip from the dark, sombre, newly-strange atmosphere of home to the bright-to-the-brimful, newly-fresh atmosphere of university without feeling like she was two different people? How did a hardened perfectionist, with a track record of impeccably high self-standards, tackle new demands when, even if she didn't realise it (and perhaps this not yet seeing it was the biggest problem of all) she was already internally pushed to her limits? Could it even be done?

I've since learnt, first as a student, and then as a teacher, that the best essay responses are those that refuse easy answers. 'YES, BUT' is one model of answer that allows room for such complexity. *Yes,* that girl was able to make it work for a time, *but* there was a demanding degree of performing required to keep the illusion functioning. She wanted to be okay so badly that she made herself look okay (even in her own eyes). *Yes,* she could, on the surface, through trying hard, appear to be okay, to be coping, to be keeping up. She could, for a while, bridge the worlds of home and away by stretching, feet splayed wide until they were uncomfortably placed in both camps. She could seem, on the surface, to be walking light, so long as she studiously avoided stepping in the shadows. *But,* seeming can only ever last for so long. Too much stretching takes its toll. Eventually the threads pull too thin, too hard, too much, and the seams break. At least, that's what I suppose, in the end, happened to me.

***

If it hadn't been for my brother's intervention, I'm not sure I would ever have even ended up at USYD, head bent over classic novels and difficult to decipher theoretical texts, sipping endless cups of tea in Manning Kiosk.

Despite all my planning and earnestness during my final school year, I had given surprisingly little thought to what came after. I'd originally put journalism at the top of my list of preferences for future study. I even had the mark I needed pasted above my desk at home, frowning down on me in rigid black and white whenever I might be tempted to slack off on my study. It paid off. I got the mark. But away from my desk, out in the real world, I questioned my decision. Did I really have what it took to be a journalist? Wouldn't my inbuilt shyness, my sensitive hesitancy, work against me in this sort of a go-get-it career? But if not that, then what? I wasn't sure. All I knew was that I wanted to do something that involved writing 'when I grew up' and, for some barely explicable reason, I had an intense, sudden desire to visit my over-the-ocean family in Holland and Canada. Gap years were common then, especially in our social circles. I knew other peers who had trips already planned to the UK or Europe, to work in schools or bars. But I had left my own idea too late to put these sorts of ordered plans into place. What could be done now?

I confessed my confusion to Greg one night, bursting through his bedroom door, just down the corridor from mine, in a flurry of words, most likely tears too. He was used to these melodramatic moments, having been through all the highs and lows of my teen years with me thus far. In fact, he was something of a secret weapon for me, always there to listen and offer advice when I believed my emotions were too out of bounds to bring to church or too messy to expose even to my friends. Greg's brotherly advice never seemed hard-edged or preachy, wrapped up as it always was in the warm embrace of empathy. On this particular occasion, he simply swivelled to face me from his desk chair by the window as I entered, turned down the music on his speaker, which was almost always playing, and listened carefully, cocking and nodding his head in his distinct thinking manner, before he responded.

'What about if you worked for six months first, here in Australia, and then you went overseas?' he proposed. 'You could still accept a position in a degree but just defer it for a year.'

He phrased it as a question, a suggestion, but really it was something of a revelation. I felt suddenly reassured, like the bits of a frustrating but alluring puzzle were fitting into place. And he had something else to say, too. He agreed with me, he didn't think a communications degree was my destiny, but he did think literature was. He thought obtaining the broad foundation of an arts degree would be the grounding I needed to take off from. This, to many people's surprise, had been his own decision a few years earlier when he met with the same post-school crossroads. Arts degrees then were not taken very seriously (perhaps they still aren't). People spoke of them as the easy road, nothing too heavy, nothing too real. On top of this, they weren't exactly considered sound financial investments. Wisdom, people argued, lay in less airy-fairy, unfocused paths. But Greg disagreed. Rather than science, where we'd always thought he'd lean, or even going straight to Bible college, he'd instead chosen to focus his attention on the highly abstract fields of poetry and philosophy. By the time I needed to make my own decision he was already deeply interested and invested in both fields. In spare pockets of hours, he was starting to write his own poems, though the extent and quality of these we would not discover for many years—nor did we know how much they would, one day, become solid anchors to us all. Literature, it turns out, is every bit as 'useful' as science; perhaps he already knew this. Greg understood my longings to write, but he believed firmly that the place to start writing was, first of all, reading. Together, we delivered the new plan to my parents, who agreed. In fact, my father, now wholly convinced, caught on with enthusiasm. I thrilled at the look of excitement in his eyes. To think that my own journey could please and excite him—could somehow even connect him more fully back to that life he'd left behind—was more than a bonus.

With the decision made, we drove into the university campus together one afternoon to make my degree deferral formal. We parked on the busy inner-city road, and Greg led me over the bridge to be met by my first hushed view of the soaring sandstone buildings, the central gothic, castle-like tower of the main quadrangle rising like a revelation from the brighter-than-green grass. As we traced our way along the paths, through archways and under old trees, you could almost smell the learning in the air. Though in the end I would stay at university far longer than my brother, for years later, I would always think of it first of all as Greg's space. He was the family explorer who discovered it, who put the flag in the ground, and I would only ever be a tourist coming after.

I worked for six months as planned, making fumbling sandwiches in a city shop, answering phones in my dad's office, and midway through the year I boarded a plane for Europe. My over-the-ocean family welcomed me with open arms and a cultural dance of three kisses; left cheek, right cheek, left cheek, or was it the other way around? that continually confused me and made me feel like the clumsy foreigner that I was. But it didn't stop me from experiencing their fondness, and my own in return. I travelled around Holland eating cake and drinking coffee (in a small cup) and beer (in a large one). I took another plane to Canada and hiked in the Rocky Mountains and drank fizzy 'pop', which I'd only ever known as soft drink, and lay carefree on my back in the grass with my cousins and watched the stars. In a strange double coincidence, I was in Paris on the day Princess Diana's car crashed, then stood outside Buckingham Palace in London several days later to place flowers against the fence, alongside thousands of others, as a mark of mourning. I have photos from that time; I am smiling as I kneel down before the floral sea of messages and tributes. But car accidents, disasters, then, were still for other people. Sure, they could strike even the likes of Royal family members in tunnels, but that didn't make them any closer to me.

Despite how much I soaked it all in, something happened while I was overseas. Now away from my normal reality, I longed to get back. Distance can have that effect. Watching all my relatives' lives in action, daily, gave me an appreciation for the familiar, organic rhythms of daily life. I felt a strong urge to return and get started with my own. But it was more than this. I saw how my relatives loved one another. I missed my Australian family. It wasn't an easy decision, but with sadness I decided to leave a month earlier than I was scheduled to come home. I didn't know then how significant that extra month would be.

On return, my family and friends waited. Emma, Katelyn, and my friend Bec came dressed as clowns, complete with wigs and white make-up, to meet me when I arrived home from the airport. Mum had organised a cake with my name on it and the message 'Welcome Home' stitched across it in chocolate fondant. That night Greg and I sat downstairs in the living room on the couch late into the night, sharing all our stories of the past six months. We exchanged new music we had discovered. I told him all the things I thought no-one would understand, all the ways my journey had brought new horizons and the faint outlines of new questions, secure in the knowledge he held them without judgement or fear.

There was more cake to come. More cause for celebration. That same December we found out my brother had passed his undergraduate honours year with flying colours and been selected for a scholarship to study postgraduate philosophy for three years. He was going to be a Doctor of the Arts. My father's latent scholar's heart was full, his son about to live a life he had never been able to. We went out shopping together and bought him a new desk. I prepared to start university alongside him. My parents glowed in the knowledge of a child returned home and finally re-finding her feet and direction and another moving on, in the best possible way, to healthy independence and the peak blooming of his potential. I re-entered church, my brother beside me to help me with any hiccups. We celebrated Christmas and New Year. We headed surely into the humid summer peak of February. Our little family ship was full of dreams and hope once more. Afloat. Full sail. And then.

And then I started university alone. I was still following in my brother's footsteps, but I could no longer see him ahead of me.

***

Katelyn and Emma were also studying at USYD, though a year ahead of me. During my first year there, they were always close by, faithful angels in boat shoes or Dr Martin boots (university life allowed you to lean into any kind of style you pleased, and though both dear friends, Em and Kate stood on opposite ends of the dress spectrum). Emma and Katelyn had been there the night I heard the news of Greg's accident; they had even stayed over at my request when I rang them later, when I didn't want to be alone. I still remember them arriving at my door, knocking gently, standing poised together on the doormat like it was a life raft they might at any moment fall off. Their hearts floated in the watery ponds of their eyes. They told me later that they almost hadn't been able to come. 'But we must,' they told one another.

Emma and Katelyn knew my story from the inside, but without my personal, particular blind spots. Perhaps this allowed them to see signs, much before I did, of my need for some extra assistance as the year carried on. So it was that one evening I found myself in a car being escorted by my friends to my first ever appointment with a psychologist. My mum had

had his name passed onto her by some well-meaning citizen. Apparently, he was very good with people my age and younger. His speciality, someone said, were those affected by sudden death. This was my first foray into the subspecialty world of mental health. I had no idea, until this time, just how many sicknesses could beset the human heart and soul.

We arrived at the address supplied to us in the dark. I had been told to enter by a side gate, as his office where he saw patients was at the side of his house. Once out of the car, I scrambled around in the bushy garden, looking for any sign of a gate-like structure. I have a terrible sense of direction, even in the light, in normal times. I can get lost going to the toilets at the shops. My friends waited patiently and parentally in the car for me to safely enter, and when I couldn't get in (which I took as a sign it was time to leave) they came out to assist me. Eventually, with their gentle prodding, together we found the gate, and even the latch, and I stumbled my way through and to the sliding glass door of the office.

The man (I can't remember his name now) was kind, softly spoken, and a lot older than I expected. Despite the separate entrance, I could still hear his wife through the wall clanging pots and cutlery as she cooked. I felt suddenly annoyed. At the noise. At the idea she might hear me. I didn't know anything about psychologists, but I thought they should at least be confidential.

'So, how are you going, Nikki?' he asked me, palms open on his lap, ready to receive anything I gave him.

'I'm fine, thanks,' I said, fists closed. Lips tight.

As he looked back at me, I felt a little guilty for not giving him anything more, but not enough to move my lips into action. All I can remember thinking is that I wanted to get home to finish an assignment due the next day. Time was ticking. I didn't want to talk about Greg with this man I didn't know. I wanted to make sure I didn't stuff up my mark in English.

Counsellors, I've since learnt, even experts, need material to work with. Like writers, they need stories, words. It doesn't matter how messy they are—the messier the better—with the raw cloth of your story they can unpick, rearrange, patch; but you need something to start with. You need to be willing to talk. I wasn't. Not yet. I told my friends on the way home that I felt uncomfortable with the noise, the house. We laughed about his wife next door. Perhaps, they suggested, we should look for someone else. I didn't return.

What could I have told him then, had I been willing to speak? About my mother who wept at night on the white cane chair in her bedroom, the one that had always reminded me of fun times, like our family holidays in Fiji. About how sometimes, when the crying was loud and strong, I held her as she clung to my back, while she wondered aloud if she could go on. About my father who watched TV downstairs, on his own, late into the night and said nothing, made no noise, nothing at all. Like a ghost, or a statue. Or about myself, dabbling in drinking (a habit I picked up in Europe) and then acting like I hadn't, going out, working, crying into my pillow sometimes only after everyone else was asleep. But waking, going to church, attending Bible study, though often so tired I lay on the floor with my head on a pillow. Or could I have asked him about the mental state of our family cat (they could analyse animal heads too, right?) who had parked himself semipermanently outside the closed door to my brother's room, the one none of us entered, nor even so much as opened a window in, for fear of disturbing the last pieces of him: the puffer on his messy bedside table, the shoes in a pile on the floor of his closet where he left them. We feared stirring even the dust in case we blew him even further way. Was that what made the cat cry and wail in a way he never had before? Did he smell the grief in the air, the pervasive, invisible scent of the emotion that couldn't yet be shaped into full sentences?

I didn't want to open that door of thought yet. Not at home. Not in some stranger's office with his wife cooking him a roast next door.

Plus, I was a Christian, right? I already had all the supports I needed. I had church, where there were always willing ears to listen to me, if I dared speak. Heck, I had a car full of compassionate friends waiting for me, willing to push aside branches on dark nights just to help make my way lighter. And I had God, didn't I? Wasn't that enough? More than enough?

University gave me structure, a focus, and a momentary feeling of normality. It also reassured me there was still something I could do. I was good at studying, good at putting words onto paper. I understood, intuitively, how to make language work for me, how to steer it in the direction I wanted it to go. I could make sense of it in a way I couldn't make sense of much else. If university reminded me also of my brother and all that we, all that he, had lost—which it did—it was in echoes and shadows. I made sure to only walk around the edges of these, to remain in the loudness of the multitude, in the light. As I learnt in my Victorian literature class, sometimes the best place to be a flaneur, to walk in disguise, is in a crowd. In a crowd, you can lose yourself for a while, even hide from yourself.

In a crowd you can ignore for a time what is impossible to forget when you are alone.

Chapter Six

Travelling Heavy

Growing up, I never thought much about the size of our family. I didn't pause to consider that some families, like ours and most of my friends, had two kids, and that others, like a boy in my class, had as many as seven kids packed into one house. I never thought, because I didn't have to, about what would happen if two kids, a pair of siblings, became, by no choice of their own, only one. And I didn't know that being the remaining one, in the same space where there had always been two, would feel like less than half of the original number.

Even before Greg left us, our house had been a quiet place. Four introverted individuals with superpowers of sensitivity and bookishness, we didn't generate much noise. Before Greg left us, this never bothered me. I didn't need to consider the virtue or not of the atmosphere of our home. It just was. After my brother died, the quiet became, paradoxically, very loud. It echoed in my ears and heart, shrilly, a shout: This is not right! But perhaps it wouldn't have mattered if there were eight or ten of us between those walls. Maybe a family who loses a member becomes, no matter its size, suddenly hollowed out and empty.

It is impossible to describe to anyone who hasn't been there just what it is like to live in such a house, in the house of mourning. Not just to visit, dropping in with some comforting words, a shower of tears (which clears again on leaving), a few tender hugs; but to move around daily in its atmosphere, one planet in a constellation of grievers. It is impossible to communicate how hard it is to exist in a familiar space that now feels like another galaxy.

Perhaps this is why around six months after my brother died, in my mid-semester winter study break, Mum, Dad, and I decided we should go away on a trip. We thought a change of scene might help. The idea began with the empty car sitting outside our house.

Shortly before he left us, my brother bought a second-hand car. Like everything else he did, he completed the job with thorough research and wisdom. Together, Greg and a friend scoured the caryards of Sydney looking for that illusive combination of economic value and reliable quality. I suppose at some point they decided they had found it, or near enough, as Greg came home proud to be the owner of his first vehicle independent of the family.

I'm not sure if Greg ever drove that car. He was the passenger in another vehicle when it collided with a tree. I've heard it said since that the road they were travelling on at the time was problematic, and that they weren't the first to meet misfortune on its cruel surface. I often think, if only they had taken another road that day, how differently it would have all turned out. Such '*ifs*' rang loud in our household for many years. *If only I… If only they… If only we…* When someone passes, especially in an unexpected, sudden way, the mourning parade includes these sorts of statements. But such discussion is, of course, as pointless as it is painful. No wishful or retrospective thinking can change the unalterable.

After the accident, that barely driven new–old car sat parked outside our house like a cruel joke, mocking us morning and night with its silence and lack of movement. It was like a physical symbol of so many things in our lives now; without my brother there was no-one to turn the key in the ignition and move forward. Eventually my parents came to a decision. We would sell the car, and with the money we would go on a trip together. Just the three of us. Together we chose the majestic South Island of New Zealand as our destination. Surely this was a fitting space to honour Greg as a family, to reflect away from the pressures of everyday life that didn't disappear, even for us; to swallow deep mouthfuls of beautiful creation.

In photos from the time, we are a tight-smiling cluster of travellers. Perhaps we even look, to the uneducated eye, like any other family on a holiday. Except that we weren't. And it didn't take long for us to discover that the old adage was true: no matter where you go, you still take yourself with you. Adding further excess to our journey baggage, each of us had not only our own sorrow to deal with and manage, but also its effect on the others. While being together was in many ways our greatest support and relief, it was also a tremendous burden. To the backdrop of pure pastel sunsets and cinematic worthy landscapes in which we sometimes did not see another person for several hours, our loss came at us full frontal, undiluted. New Zealand is a vast paradise, but it is also a quiet one. Solitude gives little space to hide. We were a delicate, fragile ecosystem, prone to unpredictable tidal shifts at any moment, riding the flux of our varied emotions. In such a way, our reality rose to the surface in those weeks, heavy and obscuring, like the fog that hung low on the road as we drove between Christchurch and Queenstown, down the southern rim of an isolated island in the Southern Hemisphere.

My parents were no doubt aware of the twin realities that faced them, as unfamiliar as the mountains that rode alongside us as we drove. They now possessed a child lost, and a child living. How did they simultaneously let go of one and hang on to the other without the equation getting confused? I was aware, too, of being in a new, uncharted position on the family map. If I were a landmark, my name might be 'the one left behind'. As I felt my own sadness descend, I also wanted to live in a way that didn't weigh them down any further. Where there were once two children—a shared responsibility—now there was only one. What if I let them down? What if I didn't *live up to* any of their dreams? Even worse, what if I somehow crushed them further? I felt both beloved and breakable, rare and precious. And they? No doubt they, too, felt the weight of still being parents of a live child. How did we all carry on this act of living when everything was so unfamiliar? What did it even mean to live now?

We fumbled through, we laughed occasionally, we sipped wine at night and one or more of us inevitably cried, we slept fitfully, we read voraciously, we visited tourist sights, we both drank in and drew back from the magnificent magnitude of it all. And, more than once, I called out my brother's name, accidentally, across our hotel room, when I meant to say Mum or Dad. Our lives might have already changed, but muscle memory was stubborn. He was with us still, even as he wasn't. In our culture, there are few grieving customs. Perhaps we needed some then. Without any guidelines, we were like grief infants. As we tottered about, clumsily pushing on the boundaries of our new reality, we wanted something to stop us falling off the edge and into the wildly beautiful, icy-sad New Zealand sunset.

One point in particular stands out from this trip, containing so much of the complexity of that time. Towards the end of our two-week sojourn, we stayed in a historic castle in Dunedin, right at the bottom of the South Island. Dunedin had long fascinated my mum, with its Scottish heritage and alluring, other-worldly appeal. An edge-of-the-earth sort of town, known for its icy breezes and majestic vistas, its art and music and university coffee culture, and its rugged, wholesome beauty, we'd been looking forward to this moment with much anticipation. Our peppy tour guide back in Sydney, who had literally stumbled over herself to help us when we told her of the reason for this trip, promised that this would be the pinnacle of our journey. I was inclined to agree; it did seem strangely appropriate. I saw significance in everything in those days. I still do. Greg loved myths and legends, C. S. Lewis and Tolkien. Growing up, Middle Earth had been like a second, imaginary home for him. He had feasted early on the tales of King Arthur. We would be doing Greg proud, I thought, by visiting spaces he would have believed in, that he would surely have visited himself had he been given a chance. So often then, I attempted to see the world through my brother's eyes, even as I used my own. As we arrived in Dunedin and made our way to the castle, the country road wound steeply upward from the water, through picture perfect green hills dotted with black-and-white cows and stone fences I hadn't seen since Ireland.

On arriving, we were shown politely to our quarters, passing on our way a younger family of four playing loudly in the castle activity room. I felt the contrast between us like a physical division as we walked on and was glad to close the door to their noise and normalcy that only seemed to amplify our difference. Inside, our room had an ornate four-poster bed and a smaller twin one I would sleep in. There was a single square window in the stone wall, framing a view of the manicured green castle garden that in almost any other circumstance would be a picture of pure joy. But as quickly and steeply as we had climbed the hills, I'd felt my high expectations and hopes descending in a way I struggled to even name.

As part of the castle experience, the family who owned it and resided there asked guests to join them for dinner in the formal dining room. Back in Sydney, this invitation had sounded exciting, and Mum and I quickly found ourselves caught up in the travel agent's enthusiasm. It would be like being on the set of a medieval movie. Up in the hills, as dusk descended and the night grew chill, our enthusiasm did not come so readily or easily. Suddenly, the prospect of our first real social engagement since the accident, with people who knew nothing about us, sent us almost into a form of communal stage fright. But we were nowhere near any other restaurants, and Dad didn't want to drive down the hills in the dark, plus my parents believed in following through on your word in a noble, stalwart way that had caused me much frustration as a kid who changed her mind easily. Dressed up and ready, the three of us crossed the chilly courtyard and knocked on the castle's heavy front door.

Inside, the dining room was warm and intimate. We were promptly seated across from our fellow travellers, mostly couples my parents' age, easy smiles on their faces, women in bright lipstick and men in pressed shirts and woollen jumpers. The first course arrived as outside the rain drizzled romantically, gently streaking the wide windows. Silver cutlery clinked while candlelight wavered. Wine glasses were topped up on emptying. I looked across at my parents, as I often did, like a protective family pet, trying to gauge a reading of their mood from the scent in the air. They seemed okay, for now. For some time, the conversation lingered safely in the confines of the last few days. Where had everyone come from, had they done both islands or just the South, did anyone plan on doing more touring after this?

When conversation shifted in less predictable directions, it was, I suppose, inevitable. A couple across from us was interested in the fact that I had just started university this year. What course was I doing? Did I enjoy it? And then, to my mother, such casual words, such innocent intentions, 'Do you have any other children?'

Of course, this is not the only time any of us has had to face this question. Even now, years later, the pathway to the answer is unclear. Even still, if someone new I meet asks if I have any siblings, my answer varies depending on the person, the relationship, the weather, my emotional state that day. *Just me, and my half siblings. Yes, I had a brother, he died. No, I had a brother.* Then, it was untrodden, untested territory. Being approached for the first time on a cold, rainy night on top of a hill in a stone castle, my parents, ever endearingly honest, simply told the truth. 'We had a son, he died five months ago.'

We returned to our room before dessert was served, crossing the drizzling courtyard silent and quick, our hands hidden in our pockets, each of us with our eyes to the path below us. The next night, instead of eating with the others, we ate peanut butter and honey sandwiches from paper plates, perched on the four-poster bed, with a view of the rolling hills framed through our bedroom window. After that we packed our bags, ready to leave again at first light.

Castle walls, like any other walls—no matter how mythical and beautiful looking, it turns out—aren't strong enough to withhold reality from storming in. And green hills, no matter how lush or inviting, are nothing compared to the fierce drought of grief and pain.

***

There is one more thing that happened during that time that I need to tell you about. It was not across the ocean in New Zealand but in the homecoming on Australian soil that the equilibrium once more shifted, catching me by surprise.

On disembarking from the plane in Sydney, we joined the tired line of travellers to catch a taxi across the city to our home in the suburbs. We asked the driver to drop me straight at church, while Mum and Dad would continue on alone. All throughout the trip, I held the warm thought close that I would soon be reunited with my friends, with normalcy. I longed for the clang and clatter of other voices and bodies around me, for the company of those for whom the world had not become so slippery and indecipherable, whose eyes did not spill tears at any unknown second. My reunion had nearly arrived, and I was ready for it. I leaned further back into the cold leather of my taxi seat, focusing on the view outside my window to pass the time. It was unusually windy that night, and the leaves in the trees sighed deep and shivered up against the telephone wires like they were trying to bend and touch them. Sitting in the back of that taxi I had a sudden, and urgent, thought. What if something happened to one of us? What if more tragedy struck? What if I were to lose one of my parents? What would I do then? On the spot, I said a quiet, fervent prayer for our safety, beseeching the Lord to protect us.

Not more than two minutes later, a tree fell down in our path, less than a metre from our car. A tall, statuesque gum tree collapsed like a giant with a sudden, freak impalement. I'd grown up among these trees. These gums were like friendly neighbours, always bobbing in the background, occasionally dropping a single branch or a bunch of leaves, but I'd never seen anything like this happen. Ever. The taxi driver had paused for a moment to check for traffic when it torpedoed into our path. 'If I had been a second later,' he said, 'it would have got us for sure.'

I took it as a sign. God had heard my prayers. He had us hemmed in. Nothing had been able to touch us. Not this time, at least. I was awed. Grateful. Startlingly aware of God's power. And also more than a little unnerved.

Whenever people dared to probe a little deeper into my faith during this time, it was usually to ask if I was angry at God. This seemed to be the main expectation of how I would be reacting, other than simply 'trusting' him. I might, they thought, like Job, be inwardly railing against God, counting all the ways he had wronged me and my family. For whatever reason, I wasn't angry, I didn't blame him. I'm not sure why. Maybe it would have been good if I'd had it out with him, face-to-face, once and for all. But I've always been averse to conflict, especially with God. One of my greatest fears in life, even before anxiety jumped into view and said, 'BOO!' is of upsetting people, of doing the wrong thing. No, I wasn't angry that my brother had died, that my parents were broken. I was, if I stopped long enough to let it come to the surface, terribly, deeply, untouchably sad. More than anything else, I felt vulnerable, tender, like a walking, barely bandaid-covered wound. This vulnerability made me extra sensitive to people's words.

For whatever reason, people say all sorts of things about God after someone dies. In an attempt, perhaps, to comfort me, more than one person had told me with serene smile, gaze lifted to the heavens, that Greg had died because God couldn't bear to live without him. I'm not sure on the theology of this. But I wasn't able to think theology then. I just thought with my feelings. My brother had loved God a lot, I agreed; he had indeed reached something of a crescendo in his relationship with his heavenly Father before he died. He seemed to understand more fully and passionately how much God loved him, and out of this sense of his own belovedness, he was loving others in a way I had not seen in the years prior. Along with his fellow Bible study leader and new friend, Rhea, he had begun more radically reaching out to outsiders, befriending, as just one example among many, a depressed young man facing potential jail time. He was going to go along to his trial with him. In my mind, I couldn't help but wander off in my thoughts sometimes and ask questions I didn't even want to ask. Was going all in for God as safe as I had always thought? If you gave him your life, as we always said in youth group, did that mean literally, your life? Was my brother's deep faith a direct cause of his death? I know it sounds illogical; there is, of course, no way of knowing why someone dies when and how they do, but at the time my mind was making these sorts of calculations. Without consciously realising it, I started to draw back a little. I kept talking to God, but I began keeping a little distance too.

There was a song we sang at church at the time based on words from Job, about how God is the one who gives and takes, but whatever happens we can still praise. It wasn't so much the words that bothered me, taken so directly from the Bible, but the nature of the tune that went with them. It was just so happy, so light, so upbeat. At some point after my brother died, I found I couldn't sing this song, and a collection of others, in quite the same way I did before. For a time, I couldn't sing it at all. The lyrics felt achingly heavy on my tongue. So I closed my mouth and bowed my head silently as those around me carried on singing.

If I'm honest, I wasn't angry at God after my brother died, but deep, deep down, I was more than a little bit afraid of him.

PART II: SUBMERGED

come peace, come
rain,
  fall in thick misty sheets
and pass,
leaving me in restful sleep,
head laid on friendly pillow to awake
    tomorrow before my dreamed of lake

it feels as though there's some treasure there
    one I'd like to find 'cause my frame can't bear
        this weight anymore.

—GVDK

Chapter Seven

Anxiety Attacks

Just as every believer has their conversion narrative, every anxiety sufferer has their confrontation story, the moment the world changed for them both internally and externally, above and below; the point in time when their relationship to everyday things, like ground, air, and most of all their own mind and body, irrevocably shifted. Electrified. Pulsed. Quaked. The moment they learnt to *fear* fear.

Despite all the drama that followed, the exact details and setting of my own confrontation were startlingly ordinary. I've since learnt this is not entirely uncommon. Anxiety thrives on stealth, on the surprise attack. Panic attacks in particular like to spring when least expected.

I was twenty years old and in my second year of university, sitting on our living room couch watching television, when PD first visited me. Of course, I knew nothing of PD's identity then, definitely not its initials. We were complete strangers, PD and me, which, I suppose, gave it even more power. The storm of anxiety came, seemingly, out of a clear-sky day, and I was suddenly in its eyeball. Mum and Dad were just up the stairs in the kitchen. I could hear them talking, their voices were not alarmed or unusual, everything was as it always had been (the altered form of 'always' since the accident, that is), but I may as well have been completely alone. I was helpless, or so I was convinced, before a force of such intense physical power, I felt like the only way to escape would be to run with all my might.

Flight.

Heat flooded my body, the muscles in my legs felt painfully tight, the sour taste of adrenaline surged up my throat. My heartbeat sped up like I was suddenly in a race car spinning out of control, off track. I felt nauseous, dizzy, sick. I wanted to make it go away. I would have done anything, *anything*, to feel normal.

Fight.

On top of all this, I felt a disconnect, like suddenly I was above my body, watching it all and unable to help myself. Except as I said, I was sitting on the couch, watching television.

My friend Sarah rang to talk, and somehow I managed to speak actual, decipherable words to her. I asked her if we could go out somewhere. Maybe, I thought rapidly (panic made my thoughts speed up), a change of scenery would help. I did not yet tell my parents anything. I didn't know what was wrong with me, but I definitely didn't want to worry them. A tiny part of me too, a part that would grow as PD and I travelled further along together, felt ashamed. Whatever was happening to me made me feel less like a young adult and more like a quivering child in danger of imminent disgrace, like she might wet her pants if she moved too much.

Sarah arrived, and we decided to go to Manly Beach, a place we both loved. Manly was a tourist mecca of fancy hotels on the water, live music and restaurants galore, and almost constant action. There was noise and distraction there, most likely crowds. Perhaps, I thought, it would be the thing to shake me out of this… whatever this was. The drive only made things worse. The winding roads, curving up the hill before the beach, took on a surreal, nightmarish quality as the sky darkened around us. Once, years ago, when we were still in high school, three boys without a licence had left in a car and ended up wrecked on the side of one of the upward bends. Memories, piecemeal, surfaced from that earlier accident. I feared we'd slip off the edge of the road, end up like those teenage boys. My seatbelt felt like a chain tying me down. I wanted nothing more than to reach our destination, to step out into the light.

After what felt like an eternity trapped in the claustrophobic setting of a Stephen King novel, we arrived. Maybe a walk would help, I thought. So we walked, of all places, to the ice cream shop on the boulevard. What more innocent and carefree destination could there be? But the terrible feelings didn't decrease, not even as we approached the cosily-lit neon sign, the long list of usually appealing flavours and delicacies painted down the wall of the building. With each step, I only felt worse. Sarah asked if I wanted an ice cream. I think I managed to shake my head. And as those around us laughed and ate triple decker cones dipped in sprinkles and took in the summer night breeze with an ease that suddenly looked totally foreign, all I could think was, *I need to go to the hospital, I need to go now. Something is wrong with me. Very. Very. Wrong.* Eventually, out of sheer desperation, all pretence of trying to appear okay dropped, and I voiced my fears to Sarah. I was sure I was either going crazy or having a heart attack. That was the first time anxiety convinced me I was breaking—not in two, but in a million little pieces, dispersed to the beach wind, flying unbound like grains of sand over the great depths of the ocean. And what was worst of all, I thought that I was the only one in the world to feel like this.

Sarah didn't take me to the hospital. Of all of my friends then, she was the savviest. She had had more than her share of suffering. She was tougher, more street smart than most other people I knew. In our latter years of high school, she'd battled her own demons and, after a time, come out on top. Her mum was a nurse. Perhaps it was no coincidence that she was the one who called that night. I'm not sure how much she knew, but she knew enough, and was gracious enough, to turn around and drive me the half hour home again, no questions asked, no complaints.

My mum met us at the door (perhaps Sarah called ahead, I have no recollection) and gave me my first dose of Valium and put me to bed. I felt a little safer, snuggled under my doona in the single bed that had been with me for longer than all the change. But I felt no less alarmed. My room was my room, but it no longer felt the same; everything around me seemed to pulse with a new energy, every opening of my eyes blinked an alarm of threat.

For days I hardly left that bed, only for the toilet, not even for a shower. Brushing my hair, caring to brush my hair, felt like a big deal. My friends visited and talked to me from the end of my mattress, which seemed like a vast distance. Occasionally, my heart lifted enough to smile stiffly at them. But the smile didn't reach to my insides, not even to my eyes. I tried, when asked, to explain how I felt. I grasped at song lyrics, like the Cranberries' 'Empty', to try to approximate meaning in the space where even words had momentarily abandoned me.

'Empty?' my friends would repeat, trying to understand, wanting me to elaborate.

'Yes, empty.' And terrified. Though I'm not sure how much I told them about that. It was almost too terrible to talk about. How could I explain to anyone else what I didn't yet understand myself? I felt trapped inside myself, inside my life, in a deep, hollow place that was filled only with the daily, often hourly, rush of fear. Like an icy mountain breeze, it swept through me, bowled me over. Whoosh. Again and again. I feared, most of all, getting lost irredeemably in this cold, lonely place inside myself that no-one else seemed able to reach, no matter how hard they tried. What if I never found my way back again?

It was Rhea, my brother's angelic co-Bible study leader, friend, and faithful companion to many ailing souls, who suggested I come with her to see a GP she knew. He was comfortable and familiar, she said, with issues like mine. Mental health was clearly not yet a word *I* was comfortable with. I still remember the pamphlet he passed over to me when I finally took my walking fear, my unwashed hair, my crumpled clothing, in to see him. It was one of those medical cartoon-type depictions made to educate the everyman about biological processes. It had this figure of a man, and all these arrows coming out from different parts of his body. At the tip of each arrow was a bodily description, and as I read through the labels, I ticked them off in my mind: *racing heart, nausea, sweating, inability to concentrate, stomach pains, feelings of loss of control, weak legs.* And then, at the top of the man, like a banner over his head, were the words that were to speak the title of a major category of my life from then on. *Symptoms of a panic attack.*

I took several weeks off university. My brain, which until now had fairly effectively planned and delivered essays, attended lectures, and operated in the world, was no longer cooperating. These previous activities seemed now to be Himalayan in demand. I wrote to my lecturers; those I couldn't contact, my friends spoke to in person. I got extensions and take-home exams organised for the future when I would be, maybe, better. I no longer cared. At last, even marks seemed meaningless, without substance. I felt nothing for them.

I wasn't exactly tired, although I slept more than ever before in this time. My limbs felt electrified. One night during that time I wrote a letter to Rhea. I don't think I ever gave it to her, but it felt good to get the feelings out. Apparently, I've since read, the act of handwriting can be therapeutic. Perhaps this is why journaling worked so well for me as one coping mechanism in the years to come. In my letter I described the anxiety primarily as physical. I felt sick all the time. Sick to my stomach. My mental state and my bodily state were so intimately intertwined, as I now know they are for many people, that ever since I have struggled whenever I become sick to not simultaneously become highly alarmed.

And I lost weight.

As a child I had been thin and wiry, my frame, like so many of Dutch origin, tall and lean, all angles and corners. As a teenager, my hormones made me fill out. By the time I was twenty-one, I weighed less than I had when I was fourteen. You would think I'd be happy. In a world obsessed with thin, my teen self certainly would have been. But I wasn't. My anxiety destabilised me. It made me feel full of air, dislodged from the earth. As I lost previous taken-for-granted confidences and capacities, I felt like I was disappearing, piece by piece. As I got thinner, I felt more and more vaporous and uncertain. I'm not sure where it came from, the weight loss. I can only conclude it was just one more way in which my body was processing pain. Several people inquired in private moments if I had an eating disorder. I didn't, but *I* was disordered.

If grief sends you back to zero, makes you start new life from the rubble, anxiety rewires your pathways, fills even the mundane with terror. After my anxiety arrived, my life looked, from my own eyes, very different. Anxiety made me live defensively, like an animal with limbs crouched, ready to pounce on any threat or thought of threat; an animal with a sore back, whose muscles were wound tight as iron. The kindly GP who showed me the stick figure pictures also helped me with something else for my real-life stick figure. He gave me a script for anti-anxiety pills.

You probably don't need me to tell you that the topic of medication for mental health is often a heated one, especially in Christian circles. How can a pill help your emotions, your moods, your insides; isn't this the terrain of

God alone? No, I don't think so. Or rather, I don't think God is anti anxiety medication any more than he is against any other medication. Not when it is approached in a considered and informed way, with reliable advice. Does knowing God mean you shake your head when someone offers you a cast for a broken leg, an injury that makes it hard to take the necessary steps of daily life without agony, without impediment? Why, then, should we malign aid for internal ailments, for chemical imbalances of the mind, for the serious, sometimes crippling effects of shock and suffering, especially when these can spread to our whole person and life? Weren't there other more natural methods I could have tried first? Yes, there were. But at that time, in that place, in my situation, I believe I needed that medication. Sometimes, medication is required just to get the energy we need to investigate and pursue other avenues of help. Later, for many years, I would try another route and go without it, pursuing the deep, hard work of counselling to get to the messages beneath my bodily symptoms, returning eventually to where I am now, unabashedly taking my little white pill daily alongside my breakfast and vitamins, alongside talking to someone when necessary. While medication isn't a replacement to God's peace, it can be, I believe, a necessary assistant to healing. As one of my future psychologists would helpfully say when I questioned the ethics of this at a later stage, 'I'm not ready to attribute Zoloft to the devil.' I took the box of pills, gratefully, when the chemist dispensed it. The only hard bit was waiting anxiously through the next few weeks to see if they would work. The body is, ultimately, a mystery. There are no guarantees. What works for one may not work for others. I prayed the pills would work for me.

Over the years, I would occasionally hear flippant remarks about living in an 'over-medicated world', about 'just needing more faith', usually by people who had no idea I was one of the walking medicated. But I would also meet, increasingly, others for whom the pills were a turning point.

In my early days of anxiety, taking pills was more of a hush-hush subject, accompanied by shame and fear of weakness and, even worse, fear that the act of taking them was an indication of a faulty faith. I did not experience this in my first bout of anxiety. I think I was too deep down in it to even have the energy to worry about this. But later on, I would hear the comments more and take them in to myself, sometimes rolling them around and ruminating on them—ironically, symptomatic of my anxiety disorder. On a bad day, when I was feeling particularly vulnerable or perfectionistic, these opinions would hurt me; on a really bad day they might make me question my own decision and even my faith. But over time, I came to see medication as coming from God's hand just as much as any other good and helpful thing: a gift, a relief and, ultimately, a way of being held.

Meanwhile, as I popped the plastic seals on my first packet of anti-anxiety medication and waited for the relief, my twenty-first birthday was rapidly approaching, and we had a decision to make. Before anxiety visited and struck me, we had already sent out invitations to a medium-sized group to attend a dinner at Bobbin Head Inn, a quaint 1930s restaurant in a national park nearby. Twenty-firsts were a big thing then in our social circle; people went all-out in elaborate parties. Mine was a toned down, more informal but nonetheless special event. There was to be an open fire. I'd told people to bring guitars to play some music. I didn't know now if I could make it. We came very close to cancelling. Even though my parents would have lost money, they were willing to do whatever it took to look after me. But something at the last minute stopped us. We should, we would, at least give it a try.

My friends came over several days ahead of the party and took me out to buy an outfit for the occasion. It was one of my first outings beyond our front door since anxiety had arrived. It felt nothing short of monumental to manage to put my feet squarely on the floor of the car. I felt unstable the whole trip, like the whirring scenery beyond the passenger window was cyclonic. Walking into the busy mall was even worse. The artificial white lights in the shops felt extra bright and the music extra loud. I remember especially the techno in one store, threatening to drill a hole right through me. I held onto handrails and leaned against the edges of counters, whatever I could find to reassure myself I would not fall. In a short time, we found shoes and a knee-length dress as well as a long skirt and top I liked. I think it was the least excited I've ever felt about making a purchase (and, I'll admit, I'm one of those girls who usually enjoys shopping—yes, the whole experience of it—but not then).

On the day of the party, my friends once more came over to help me get ready for the event. Sarah, who had been with me during my confrontation, did my hair in probably the most elaborate style I've ever had. In an act of loving friendship, she threaded my hair with dozens of small roses. I felt like a (slightly alternative, Maid Marianesque) princess. I'm not sure what happened, but now with my new hair and clothes on, heading out to my special night, something switched back on inside me. For a night, it was as if I were under a Cinderella spell, or perhaps it was something far more holy. Not a fairy godmother, but a heavenly Father, switching on all the fairy lights for a kid who needed a break but who was too momentarily broken to ask, or believe, in any more than what she had. I felt well. I sat and joked with my friends, who made beautiful speeches that pulled laughter from a forgotten space inside me. One friend from uni, who I hadn't seen since I'd left for my recuperation, met me at the door and proceeded to fold me into the tightest hug I've probably ever received, before or since. It was almost embarrassingly tight, and long, as if he were trying to squeeze all the pain out of me, to shake it free. For a moment, I felt held. And not just by my young, caring friend.

The medication, it appeared, also did its part. Two weeks passed and I started to feel a little better. And then, a little bit more. Perhaps, as one professional later suggested, this had just been a delayed grief response. If so, I could now head back into life. I did my exams late, at home. The next semester, I tentatively walked back out into the world.

If you have a panic attack once or only ever so often, it remains in the attack category. If you have them multiple times or spend your whole time not having one thinking about how scared you are to have one again, it's called a disorder. It appeared I was in the second category. But being the perfectionist I was, I wanted a better result than that. As I emerged from my blur, which in many ways had numbed me to anything but my immediate desperation and desire to feel better, old feelings returned. Guilt. Shame. I could see how much it hurt my parents to see me like this, even though they offered me nothing but love, support, and acceptance. But even their love made me tender. They had already lost one child; they didn't need to lose another. Not in this way. Not simply fading away. So, I strove to reclaim a new form of order. I began again.

I redoubled my efforts to make up for lost time. Like a bird with an injured limb, I flapped and fought my hardest to get traction. But all the while, on the tip of my wing, just out of eyesight, the injury remained.

Chapter Eight

Falling from the Sky in the Year 2000

It was the end of 1999, the eve of the year 2000. Y2K frenzy filled the air. Some worried about computers seizing up or planes falling spontaneously from the sky. My own concerns were much smaller and far closer to home. I just wanted to get out of bed each morning, to put my feet squarely on the ground and walk into the new day. If I could only keep on going, I told myself, perhaps I could leave all the horror of the last few months behind me, buried in the dust of times past, smoothed over by determination and a new orientation. I looked to the future wearing blinkers of hope. What better time for a fresh start than a new millennium?

And what better place to begin again than half a world away. Less than six months after anxiety first gnashed its jagged jaws and swallowed me whole, I found myself spat out on the opposite side of the globe again. My parents and I had decided to spend the holiday season in the Northern Hemisphere, hoping for a white Christmas, or at least a less sun-beaten one, and to reunite with my father's family, most of whom we hadn't seen since the accident.

We visited England first and celebrated the Christmas season in Cambridge, the dreamy university town made even dreamier bedecked in the external trappings of festivity. We pressed ourselves close into the cosy, candlelit corners of pubs, where the light danced jigs on stone and wood, drinking in the fairytale smells made by real pine Christmas trees, so unlike the cantankerous, artificial one we'd left in its box at home. On Christmas Eve, we walked by a long line of hopefuls camped outside Kings College chapel, waiting to breathe in the wonder of the choir singing 'The Messiah'. Just passing close to it brought a feeling of almost holy expectation. On Christmas Day, we ate roast turkey and cranberry sauce from bone china plates in the hotel restaurant, consuming a bottle of champagne organised ahead by a friend in Sydney, and afterwards we walked along the Cambridge River, scarves wrapped tight around our necks, our cheeks kissed red by the wind. Only as afternoon bumped early into evening, dusk descending over day like a rough wool blanket, did I sometimes feel the now familiar jolt of electricity enter my body, the precursor to panic and fear. I tried my hardest to shake it off, like the trees shook off the snow—or I imagined they would, if it had only decided to fall for us.

We were glad to move onto my father's homeland, where our relatives loved on us in slices of apple cake and cream. While my parents and half-sister Michelle's family celebrated in her living room with traditional Dutch fondue, I brought in the new year in the middle of Amsterdam with my cousins and about a million other extremely tall nationals, dancing in what felt like a forest of human trees. Renegade fireworks exploded incessantly, sending an unending stream of smoke and noise into the air. It was unbelievably crowded and noisy for a kid from the Sydney suburbs, who only half a year earlier had dreaded even leaving her bedroom. But I drank it all in, alongside the multiple refills of beer, and in the early hours of the new century I collapsed on a mattress on the floor between my two cousins.

Despite all the necks craned and watching across the world, no planes fell from the sky. Not yet. To my knowledge, the computer brains kept ticking.

But the year 2000, it turned out, was to be a sky-dropping year in other ways for me and my family.

***

About thirty-six hours after we disembarked in Sydney, my mum came into the family room to find me. My father was already back at work and had left before I even woke from my jet lag-confused slumber. It was just us, and the late morning movement of light and shadow in the quiet house. I stretched and looked up from the book I was reading.

'I think I might need to go to the doctor,' my mother said, almost under her breath.

I startled. And not just at the words themselves. My mum almost always modulated her voice to a polite cheerfulness, but her tone, though quiet, was heavy. She didn't look quite right either. Her usual bright lipstick was missing, her lips dry. Her face was pale, even taking into account our very recent global travel.

'Why?'

'My chest hurts.'

'How long has it hurt?' I asked, my own chest registering a flutter, a disturbing quickening.

'Most of the night.'

'Why didn't you tell me earlier?' I pressed. 'Wait, did you tell Dad?'

I didn't have to hear the answer to know. 'I didn't want to be a bother,' she would say, she did say. My mother was close to a mute angel when it came to voicing her own needs.

Which made this all the more serious.

We readied ourselves as efficiently as we could. I changed out of my pyjamas, pulling on the first clean clothes I could find. Our suitcases still sat clustered together in the hallway, not yet stored away.

Together we took a taxi to our local family doctor's practice, a white brick building with a large, central bay window on a quiet cul-de-sac. I stood to the side while my mother lay on the examination table and the doctor took her vitals, including an ECG, and made a phone call, not quite able to keep the siren shrill of emergency from her voice as she did so. The cardiologist on the other end of the line did not hesitate in her response. 'Get that woman in an ambulance. Now.' Mum, it appeared, had managed to suffer a heart attack in near secrecy. Perhaps when your heart has already been broken, any pain that follows is relativised.

In the ambulance we were surrounded by people. In the hospital I was alone. While my mother's chest became a foreign tentacle-land of tubes and monitors, I sat, impatient, on an emergency department plastic chair. I rang Katelyn, and she and Nathan, her older brother and one of the Fellas, came to sit with me and then, as the hours wore on, take me back to their family's home close by. We watched television absently, and they offered me food while we waited for my dad. For news of my mum. I wasn't hungry. Fear filled the empty cavern of my stomach, and it had a sound, a persistent urgent ticking, like a bomb waiting to go off.

At last, news came in. The prognosis was sobering but hopeful. My mother would need a stent inserted inside her chest, and until then she would need to stay in intensive care.

I returned to the hospital to see her once more. She was fifty years old, and she looked impossibly small and still in the white medical bed, her body drowned in the nondescript hospital gown. My own chest ached to see her there, perhaps because I didn't just see her there, with her broken heart in need of fixing. I saw the last few years there too, pressing down in the tangle of chords, beeping incessantly like the orange lights of the machines, pulling her into its web.

We still don't know why Mum's heart broke at that time, whether it was triggered by the long flight home or whether it was more like my anxiety, a delayed reaction to everything that had come before. Soon after her surgery, which was, thankfully, successful, we discovered she also had a life-altering autoimmune disease. She has required multiple treatments and medical interventions to cope with the daily struggle of living in her own body ever since. She has borne them all bravely.

Many years later, as Mum recounted her complex medical history to a new specialist, the doctor asked her a question, 'Did you have any major life events prior to the onset of all this?' He asked it slowly, gently, in a way that made her feel heard.

When she told him her story, he was hardly surprised.

Intense shock and suffering aren't just reserved for the mind, nor does pain always spill out clear from the tear ducts, released and forgotten. Suffering can lodge, hidden, inside your body for long periods, manifesting in weird and wonderful physical ways. As the excellent book of the same title says, no matter how hard you try, *The Body Keeps the Score*.

Pain and loss contributed, at least in part, to the breaking of my mother's heart. To the weakening of her body. And mine? I thought if outside events could just calm down for a while, if the world could just give us a break, eventually my anxiety would follow. I still believed, or wanted to, that there was a way to not just learn to live with anxiety, but to escape its web altogether.

***

'Hi, Nikki, sorry to wake you.'

It was several months after my mum returned home from the hospital, and we had all been busy attempting to regain our old 'normal' again—or what we believed to be normal—when a phone call pierced the night air. It was midnight, my parents were asleep in the room next door, so I picked up the receiver, groggy and disoriented. One of my uncles was on the other end of the line. It took me a moment to place him as we didn't speak often, and definitely not in the middle of the night.

'I have to speak to your parents.' His voice was strange, surreal almost. Once more, my heartbeat hit the accelerator.

My aunt, my mother's youngest sister, a popular, vivacious high school English and legal studies teacher, was being rushed to a hospital emergency department.

'Can you come?' my uncle continued to my equally sleep-hazy parents.

My uncle had asked for Mum and Dad, so I'm not entirely sure why I decided to get in the car with them too. Perhaps I just didn't want to be left alone in the middle of the stunned night. Sometimes knowing is better than not knowing. The imagination can be capable of more damage than the eyes. But I think the real reason I came with them was the same reason I cringed every time I feared something, anything, would hurt them. I was playing emotional bodyguard, wanting to buffer my parents in any way I could from yet another onslaught of suffering.

We sat in a private waiting room with my cousin, my aunt's only son, and my uncle, until the doctor came to bring us news. It was a tiny room, like a holding space or a jail cell, square, blank-walled, and uninviting. Untouched magazines sat on a small table, like a sorry pile of building blocks no child wanted to play with. The hours moved infinitely slowly.

'I'm sorry,' the doctor said as he appeared at the doorway at last. I remember his hair was smooth and neat, but his face was crudely impassive.

'She's dead.' He said it straight out, like he was informing us the item we had ordered on the hospital cafeteria menu was no longer available. The words hit the air like an assault. So much for my being any kind of buffer or bodyguard; the bullets had let fly before I'd even scanned to look for their arrival.

We were allowed in through the curtained-off cubicle to say goodbye to her. I brushed my hand briefly across the top of her soft, short, reddish-brown hair, unable to comprehend what had just taken place while we were lying, unknowing, in our beds.

We never found out the exact reason for my aunt's death, only that she had had what looked like a severe stomach bug in the hours before she dropped into unconsciousness. The coroner's report was inconclusive. Anxiety thrives on uncertainty, feeds on delicious morsels of mystery. Perhaps that is why, for years and years after, whenever my stomach hurt, whenever I felt a hint of nausea, even a sway of dizziness, anxiety was quick to tag along too, pulling hard on my sleeve, whispering dire predictions in my ear, over, and over, and over again: 'What if you have the same thing as your aunt did? I mean, we never really found out what it was. What if it's genetic? What if it will soon be your time too? How will your parents cope then? Will you be able to protect them, will you? Will you?'

As was so often the case any time a new threat emerged and took hold of my thinking, anxiety's supportive wing-person, vigilance, stood up, squared its shoulders, and declared its precautionary promise of protection: 'Just in case, I will stay awake. Just in case, I will watch for any hints of danger. Just in case, I will never let down my guard.'

The voice of vigilance might sound like it is being helpful. 'Just in case' might feel safe, temporarily, but, let me tell you from many years of experience, just in case is an exhausting place to camp out and stay.

***

Not everything that fell from the sky in the year 2000 was bad.

He carried a backpack. He looked like he was going on adventures. That's what I always say first when people ask how I met my husband. I do not tell of his gum tree–grey-green eyes, and the way he leant forward gently from his tall height to match himself to the size and situation of anyone he was with. Nor about the way we could talk for hours without faltering, or how our conversation led us down wild, unexpected tracks of mutuality and understanding. And laughter. I sometimes mention, from the safe distance of time, how I chased him down, unashamedly, until he noticed me. Thankfully, he took it from there. But I blame the backpack he wore everywhere he went. Something about it intrigued me, pulled me in. I sensed he was going places, and I wanted to go with him.

They swapped bags once many years ago, my not-yet-husband and my brother, when their overnight luggage got mixed up at our church. Mike did not know the older youth group leader Greg, with the single, defiant hoop earring, who read philosophy and played the drums. Greg did not know the young teen with the hair in his eyes who was good with a skateboard and guitar and hadn't yet discovered his own formidable capacity for thought and making music with words. Their identical carry bags changed hands, before they were once again reunited with their original owners. I like to think of it as a form of symbolic exchange. The bag a journey metaphor. One day there would be another exchange. I would no longer travel alongside my brother. But I would travel alongside Mike.

That night in the small hospital room in the year 2000, as we waited nervously for news of my aunt, in an attempt to think of other things, I turned my thoughts to a wedding I was invited to the next day with my new, backpack-wearing boyfriend; the one I already sensed, somehow—perhaps like my parents did, all those years before—that I would spend my life with. The wedding was to be held up the coast, by a lake, at a peaceful place where water met sky. I phoned Mike to tell him the night's news in the morning.

'I'm so sorry,' he said. 'That's awful. Don't think you have to come today. They'll understand, of course they will. Nobody will mind at all if you need to stay home and rest.'

I didn't need to see his face to know he meant what he said. We'd only been dating a few months, but empathy was one of Mike's major character strengths. He felt the shock through the phoneline, like it was physical. But the problem was that I minded. My new relationship with this boy who seemed to intuitively understand me had already become a strong point of stability, of comfort, in a world that was increasingly revealing itself as anything but. I wanted nothing more, especially right then, than to be by his side.

'If it's still okay, I want to come,' I said, almost shyly, a little afraid, perhaps, of my own intensity.

That afternoon, as we drove out of Sydney and up the freeway towards the coast, together with Mike's younger brothers, Rich and Chris, I felt the brevity of life in the wind rushing through the open windows, saw the outline of sorrow on every leaf edge, the sadness latent in every cloud. But I turned my cheek the other way and leaned into the laughter that filled the car, the freedom of a group of brothers who had not yet lost one another, the casual confidence of a family who hadn't yet hurt as mine had.

As we stepped out at our destination, I tuned out the horror and listened instead to the hope all around me, until I didn't just stand on the outside of it, looking in, but let myself become swallowed into it, a part of the festivity and celebration. And all that long afternoon and evening, I held Mike's hand tightly. Tighter, perhaps, than I had ever held anything else before. Tight enough to feel the ache every time I needed to let go.

***

Growing up, my brother and I were both hopeless romantics, despite the fact that neither of our forays into teen relationships had had any more than a short-lived duration. By the time Greg was twenty-two and I nineteen, neither of us had yet found the 'one', no matter how much we dreamed of and yearned for the day we would. When I was overseas, we exchanged letters, amongst other subjects, about our failed love lives. During this time Greg sent me a poem, called 'Rain', that he had composed down at the South Coast holiday shack of his friend Scott, a place he loved to go and feel at peace. *It's completely fictional*, he wrote to me. *All in my imagination.* But the picture he painted seemed so real. It touched me then, even as it remained a mystery.

> rain
> > is your hand in mine when all the world hurts,
> > rain is your arms of soft sadness around my waist
> > wrapping me in cardigan sheers of sweet comprehension.

I recorded these words in my journal, four years later: *I think I have met the character from 'Rain', Greg. His name is Mike. And he's amazing.* Perhaps in writing it down, I felt like I was telling it to my brother, sharing the news I knew he'd love.

Although Mike never met Greg, the attachments were still there, in other ways beyond the mistaken bags. Mike's mum and his younger brother

Chris were at Greg's funeral. Chris had heard Greg speak at the youth camp he was on: the last time, in fact, Greg spoke publicly. They came home and told the rest of their family about the girl who loved her older brother so much it hurt to watch. Mike later inherited Greg's weighty collections of philosophy and theology books and found the first leads for his future writing and research projects on Reinhold Niebuhr in amongst their pages.

And he loved Greg's sister well.

With Mike, I shared more of my feelings about the past few years than I had with anyone else, more than I'd told my parents, my extended family, even my friends. And he listened. One night, when I was so overcome with emotion that audible words couldn't come, he sat on my bed beside me as I cried, and we wrote notes back and forth to each other on a piece of paper. I kept that paper for many years, the wallpaper of words testament to the fact that Mike opened up things inside me that no-one else could.

He pulled the hidden tears out of me too.

One day when we were dating, he was late coming over to pick me up, and I was on my own at home waiting with too much time to think, the emotions building and building, so that when he at last arrived they burst forward like a flood, and I fell into his chest, wordlessly weeping.

'I'm sorry,' I said through heaves. 'I just can't seem to stop.'

While many other twenty-year-olds might have run for the hills, or at least the end of the street, he didn't even ask for an explanation. He just held me, stroked my back, and touched the top of my head, gently, as my tears wet his shirt. The more he listened, the more I kept going, siphoning my sorrow between us until it became a shared river.

And it wasn't always and only tears. We exchanged laughter too, our senses of humour fitting together like two pieces of a jigsaw, bouncing off one another naturally. We watched comedy together, went for walks hand in hand, read books, listened to music, drank coffee, cooked our own recipe of bruschetta late at night in my parents' kitchen. We shared our dreams, mine of writing, and of someday owning a retreat where hurting people could visit, and his of ministry and theology. In a very short amount of time, the spot tucked in beneath his chin, or beside him in the car, or sitting across from him at a coffee shop, or reading beside him at a library, became my home.

And so it was I developed my greatest new love and my greatest new fear simultaneously. I loved my new life partner. I also feared losing him. The two feelings, intense love and intense fear, were so intertwined it was very hard to separate them. A new series of 'what ifs' marched in with our relationship, the largest and loomiest of all: what if something happened to pull us apart, what if we broke up? I didn't know if I could handle another separation, even one that was earthbound. My nervousness about even the possibility of this made me ask often and persistently for reassurance. Anxiety likes reassurance, so does young love; the two together are a potent combination.

'Are we okay?' became one of the repeated refrains of our relationship, putting hidden pressure on even the best of days.

Two young university students with stars and metaphors in our eyes, we married three years after we first met, me with a ring of flowers on my head, he with a new haircut and wearing a suit. (One of the few times in life he's worn one. Academics don't do formal.) Our friend and minister, Justin, officiated at the church, and we chose the Psalms as our focus texts, with all their complex truth about life's realities and God's unquenchable steadfastness. Candles flickered, live jazz played, and the sun set over the Pacific Ocean, metres away from our reception venue. My bridesmaids were the same girls who had stood beside me the last five years of grieving and anxiety. Mike's brothers and sister joined our wedding party. No detail was spared. It was an exquisite opening to our union, the first step in a lifetime of steps.

But it was only the first step. And we were only at the beginning of our journey together.

Romantic, soul-mate love is undeniably a beautiful thing, as we all celebrated that night, but it doesn't dissolve the problem of pain, no matter how much we want it to or try to make it; and believe me, I tried. Leaving and cleaving is one thing. Wanting to escape, while clinging white-knuckled tight to another human being, no matter how wonderful, no matter how much you enjoy keeping close, is never your answer to a flourishing life. We discovered this as early on as our honeymoon.

In the very weeks when everything should have been as perfect as a Disney dreamscape, an uninvited guest turned up to crash the party. Anxiety, with a whole load of baggage I never planned on packing, barged on in.

Chapter Nine

In Health and in Sickness

We didn't so much choose as simply accept that we would recite traditional prayer book vows in our marriage ceremony. It was just the way it was done in our Anglican church. We'd witnessed dozens of couples run their tongues over the somewhat archaic-sounding phrases, words like 'honour' and 'protect', following the thread of ceremony until they closed their union in a kiss. Looking back now, I'm a little surprised that we didn't contemplate, if even for a moment, writing our own, personalised versions. We were both definitely capable of it. But I was so keen to get married, I would have read from the back of a chip packet if someone asked me to. Plus, I liked to play by the rules. Sprouting subjective love poetry would most likely have been met unfavourably, if not outright rejected. That was saved for other mediums, like music. Like the James Taylor songs we chose for our processional and recessional, a tribute to my brother and his vast CD collection. When the microphone was held out before us by our pastor, we repeated the words he told us, line by line, formalising our union with well-worn, centuries-old phrases.

I suppose we knew what we were saying in the echo, but did we really take it in, did we weigh the words in our hearts, consider the implications as we said them?

Understandably, I didn't want to dwell too long on the ''til death do us part' part. With my family's very recent history, I didn't go anywhere near the vicinity of considering this possibility in our beginning. But what about, 'in sickness and in health'? Have you ever noticed that sickness actually comes first, leads the sentence? Why, then, do we so brashly brush past it, hastily heading for health, like it's the almost certain, the expected, destination? The young, especially, think of sickness like an afterthought, an aberration. Health is what we highlight, what we expect. Health is what we want to ride into the sunset with. I wanted it just like everyone else, perhaps more fervently than ever in this new phase of life. In this way maybe I did write my own vows, after all, but silently. In my own head. For where is happily ever after ever written into the prayer book version? And yet, that's what I was thinking about, anticipating, as I looked into the sparkle of my husband's grey-green eyes, as I held his large, warm hands, so capable of holding me secure, as we pressed our lips together to the sound of cheers, to the embrace of applause.

The muscles of my mouth made the shape of the words 'in sickness', but perhaps what I meant, what I longed for most of all was something more along the lines of 'in success and in health' than the original meaning.

***

We agreed early on we'd spend our honeymoon in New Zealand. Since that first complicated trip with my parents, I'd actually travelled several times to the land of lakes and mountains, of glaciers and quaint accents. Mike's family were Kiwis. He'd lived in Auckland until he was eight years old when his dad's job called them to Sydney. A loyal All Blacks rugby supporter, his love for his home country ran deep. It seemed only natural we'd return to this special place for our first adventure together, just us. And like the soaring peaks of the New Zealand alpine mountains, our hopes for our time there together were high.

The South Island city of Christchurch was obligingly beautiful and clear skied as we stepped out of the airport the morning after our big day. The crispness of the air felt cleansing to our tired eyes. I'd prepared for the wedding, perhaps over-prepared, right down to the colour and size of the pew bows. What I hadn't prepared for was the feeling of exhaustion that came afterwards. By the time we departed the reception venue to the sounds of cheers and waves, I felt both jubilant and stunned. We found our hire car parked and ready for us outside the airport, a quaint little jeep Mike had chosen with a clear plastic roof that we could unroll when the weather was fine, letting the light and air pour in. I curled my feet up underneath me on the high passenger seat, and as I looked out the window through the path of light, I let myself imagine, like I had already been doing for weeks, all that now lay ahead.

We'd planned our dream trip from my family's computer. We thought we were smart and savvy, putting our limited budget to good use. We clicked the mouse and peered at tiny, poor-quality pictures of bedrooms and kitchenettes. When one motel alluringly promised 'honeymoon suite' at an affordable price, we let ourselves believe the elaborate promises and enticing phrases included in the brief description.

Our accommodation, it seemed, was further from the centre of town than I had expected. We pulled into the motel carpark and searched the line of identical doorways and low, boxy brick exteriors for any clue to the exact location of the little spot of Christchurch that was to be our home-away-from home for the next few days, our space to unwind and refuel and harmoniously become one. Nothing stood out. Perhaps, we thought, there was something we were missing.

When no-one immediately came to meet us, we rang the bell on the desk in the small, nondescript motel reception, quickly realising that the problem wasn't with our eyes, or the angle at which we were looking, but with the reality itself.

It is hard to adequately describe the effect of entering our 'honeymoon suite' for the first time. A corner room overhanging the carpark, differentiated from all the other rooms only by the small set of concrete stairs leading up to it, the suite wasn't so much sweet as a shock. 'Disappointing reality-check' might do to explain it. 'Appalling imposter' might be another way of saying it. 'Not at all what we expected' perhaps sums it up best. As we opened the door to the new chapter of our lives together, the sight that met our green, impressionable eyes was less of a vision and more of an affront.

The room itself was small and boxy, miles away from how the photos had made it look (hello, deceptive use of lens). The kitchenette was windowless and no more than a metre and a half wide, so that when you stood in it you felt like you were preparing food inside a pantry (and not a butler's pantry), and the view was not so much scenic, as of a scene. From a tiny concrete balcony that hung suspended over the asphalt like a building-site crane, we had the perfect view… of the carpark. But perhaps the worst bit of all was the bed. Set in the middle of the room, like the centrepiece it should have been, it was hard to miss. But not in a good way. Garish sheets—the sort that had the sheen of silk but were definitely not silk and, on closer inspection, looked and felt exactly like plastic—wrapped the mattress in lurid purple.

Always sensitive to my surroundings and aesthetics, the room came to me not as an embrace but as a slap.

All of this, of course, would have been eventually bearable, perhaps even funny, once the shock settled in, except for what happened on that first night of our honeymoon—and beyond.

***

We decided to walk into the town centre for dinner. If we couldn't enjoy our room quite as much as we'd anticipated, there was still a whole city to take in. I pulled on a new dress bought for the occasion and tied my hair back in my preferred style then, a loose bun. Mike changed his shirt and splashed on a small amount of the cologne he'd worn through our dating years. The late dusk light felt good on our faces as we walked, with the added effect of drawing out some of the words we hadn't been able to find in the close atmosphere of the room.

'It's all going to work out fine,' Mike said. 'And if not, there's always the next place. It should look extra good after this.'

I laughed, too glad to be outside again to stay angry.

It didn't take us long to find a restaurant we liked the look of, busy enough to attest to its quality, but not too busy as to overwhelm us or swallow our new-found words. The decor was modern, not usually our style, but the menu seemed creative. Lines of wine bottles hung above the bar in glass cabinets like an art installation. My new husband was something of a foodie. He knew how to combine flavours like he knew how to play guitar, where I was tone deaf. Then, as now, I deferred to him when it came to ordering.

The meals, when they arrived, did not disappoint, especially not when combined with the New Zealand red Mike chose to accompany them. Much like the walk, the wine seemed to be helping, loosening my tongue, easing the tightness at the base of my shoulders. I took another sip, and then another, remembering the words of an older friend at church; one who, as far as I knew, rarely drank. 'A little alcohol isn't a bad idea to loosen up on your honeymoon.' It was almost biblical. By the third glass, I was feeling not so much lightheaded as simply light, airy, relaxed. I looked ahead to the night that followed with anticipation. Just as I was wondering how it would all play out, I remembered something else. In the disappointment of arriving in the room, and the effort to get ready to go out, I'd forgotten to take my birth control pill, the one the doctor had said needed to be taken at roughly the same time each night to be effective (and at this very early stage of our marriage, 'effective' was something of a priority).

'Quick,' I said to Mike, sharply shifting the atmosphere. 'We need to get back to our room. Now!'

The words in themselves sounded good, of course, bearing in mind our context, but the reasoning wasn't exactly what we had been hoping for.

The night was now cold, and we half speed-walked, half ran home. It wasn't a short walk; as I said, our motel was quite some distance out of town. The heavy meals slugged around in our stomachs alongside the wine. By the time we arrived home, our feet were tired and sore, and our moods considerably dampened.

I took the pill with a glass of water. We lay down beside one another.

It must have been only a few minutes later that I started to feel sick. I leant into the faux silk/plastic pillows, trying to stay as still as possible, to will my body to stop rocking.

'I think I'm going to throw up,' I said to my new, now shirtless husband, hovering above me surfing channels on the TV in an effort to distract me from my discomfort.

'You'll be okay—' he leant in close to reassure.

'No!' I pushed him roughly out of the way and stumbled the short space to the bathroom, making it just in time to lean over and wretch.

Sickness, it seemed, had expediently arrived.

I'm not sure if it was an extreme case of one-flesh-empathy or a result of the shock of seeing me throw up for the first time and holding my hair back as I did it, or whether it was simply something we both ate or drank, but the next moment Mike was bent over as well.

Eventually, from sheer exhaustion, our bodies spent from their ordeal, we collapsed beside one another in our shiny purple cocoon.

I'd like to say the next morning I woke up and felt better and we continued on our merry way, as if it never happened. But that would be a lie. And I promised you at the beginning that I'd tell you the truth: the good, the bad, and the very dream-crushingly ugly. The next morning, when I woke, my husband was still faithfully beside me, his long arm draped securely around the circle of my waist. But something else was there too. PD, like a debt collector, perched alert and watchful on my pillow.

At first, I tried to fight it in any way I could think of. I thought that if I could just distract myself enough, maybe the snarky-elf-on-my-shoulder that was anxiety would go away. I made breakfast in the windowless kitchenette and sang praise songs out loud in the small echoey space to try and lift myself out of myself. It didn't work. I got dressed carefully and stared into the mirror, taking in my freshly manicured nails, my expertly shaped eyebrows and my darkly tinted lashes, all deliberate preparations for the wedding, and the only occasion I've ever done all three before or since. I'd never looked better. A young woman in the peak moment of her life, never more loved. Maybe, I thought, if I could just try and see myself how the outside world might see me, I'd feel better inside too. It didn't work. Anxiety was still there.

After breakfast we headed out for a gentle exploration of Christchurch's main square, hoping to take in some of the history, and peek into some of the artsy stalls and stores I'd read about. This was Christchurch before the

2011 earthquake that would decimate and shake its centre. All was calm and quiet, as cosy, serene, and welcoming a city as anywhere. Even so, I don't remember entering a single doorway. My only clear recollection is of standing outside the cluster of elegant stone buildings, frozen on the spot, with such strong surges of adrenaline I feared I would collapse where I stood, in a desperate, deflated honeymoon-heap.

'I need to go back to the motel room,' I told Mike urgently. The motel room that didn't live up to its grand name, that just walking into filled me with disappointment, but that was preferable to this feeling of complete overwhelm, to this out-of-control hysteria. It wasn't a request or even a preference. It was a plea.

***

'What do you think?' Mike leant down and touched the smooth porcelain of the bathtub, breathing in the scent of the flowers perched elegantly in a vase on a stool beside it, and turned back to face me. 'Should we try it?'

This time our accommodation hadn't lied. Moving on from the honeymoon suite from hell had brought us, at least it appeared, to a far better place. The pinnacle of our trip was a unique location called The Lazy Fish. Back in Sydney, as we scoured the screen for creative ideas, this one had stood out, a concession to the tropical island glitz we avoided, but a laid-back, alternative version that promised no technology, astounding views, board games on the wide verandah, and hessian-styled hammocks to swing in while reading books or dreaming the day away. True to its name, the retreat-style accommodation floated pleasantly at the top of the South Island. It required a water taxi just to get you there.

And our room came with the luxury of a private, outdoor, claw-foot tub.

A soft sprinkle of rain was starting to fall, folding us into a gentle, misty quiet as we stood like two intrepid explorers before the bathtub. I huddled into my rain jacket, pulling my hood over my hair, and considered the view for a moment. The overhanging branches of the large trees protected us a little, and the grey steel-like colour of the water in the distance was almost majestic as the rain rolled in.

This was finally the stuff honeymoon fantasies were made of.

Adventure, I knew, would say yes to my husband's question; spontaneity would gladly take the risk. Once-in-a-lifetime-honeymoon-high would jump right in with champagne and extra bubbles. But anxious-wife-with-fear-of-imminent-catastrophe wanted to stay inside. I chose for *us* both to go back inside. And my husband didn't complain, not once, as he put his hand on my back and closed the door behind us, and together we looked out on the stillness of the rainy night.

And in the silence, alongside the falling of the rain, I thought of all the ways I was failing—and ever so early—in the lead role in my own dream.

***

While I lay in our four-poster bed the following morning, my stomach upset once more, my husband asked the staff, a group of gregarious young women who oversaw The Lazy Fish, if it was possible for me to see a doctor.

'Not here,' they joked, incredulous. 'The nearest medical centre is in town, you need to take the water taxi across to the land and go from there, but your stay doesn't end for another night.'

To their obvious confusion, perhaps even derision, we cut our stay short and took the water taxi back to land the next afternoon, driving through some of the most beautiful scenery I've ever seen. Green hills, Psalm 23 stuff, the outside world was the epitome of peace. Why then, I asked myself, couldn't I feel peace inside? It's one thing to be able to blame the environment for uncomfortable feelings. In a war zone, for instance, everything I was experiencing would have made sense. But in accommodation of this calibre, surrounded by nothing but comfort, it didn't seem to add up at all. This frustrated me further, super-charging me with guilt. If there wasn't something external to blame, all that was left was me. It was my fault I was feeling this way, and that my feelings were dictating so much of our direction. We'd barely embarked on the happy-ever-after, and I'd already stifled it with my pain.

We found the hospital with the medical centre attached.

A young male doctor in a white coat took us into a consultation room, and Mike and I sat beside each other. I stammered out my story in broken pieces: the initial night of sickness, the weakness following, the queasy, uneasy feeling ever since that I couldn't seem to shake.

'Have you taken a pregnancy test?' he asked after I told him my symptoms.

'No, I'm not, I mean, that is, I can't be,' I tried to reassure him.

'But you could be,' he said.

'No, I'm not—'

'Take a test anyway.'

How could I tell him that the very factors that brought me in there, sickness and fear, were keeping us from any such possibility? I felt stupid and young. Inexperienced and naive. In the end I took the pregnancy test just to make him stop talking. It came back negative, of course.

The doctor sent me away with very little in the way of explanation and a prescription for some anti-nausea tablets. The tablets, at least, took some of the unsettling sensations away. Everywhere we went after that, I made sure they were held securely in my handbag or pocket.

They helped, and they didn't.

While they made me feel more secure, they also made me feel fragile. Dependent. Faulty. Like I was broken, beyond being able to fix myself. A bad wife. A bad Christian wife. Perhaps, even, a bad believer.

We mightn't have written our own vows, but we were certainly living them now, in all their rugged, earthy particularity.

The ink of our signatures on the marriage certificate had barely dried before our new bond was being stretched and pulled in ways that nobody, not even us, could have predicted.

Chapter Ten

Secrets

Technically, we didn't go into our marriage entirely uninformed. In the weeks and months before our wedding, we underwent what was called 'marriage preparation' or 'prep', a form of premarital counselling the church offered to ready us for our union. Our particular preparation was steered by an older minister called Joe, one of the softest, kindest individuals I've ever had the pleasure of meeting, before or since. Joe was small, probably less than five foot five, and had soft, curly white hair, like wool. He possessed in equal measures the voice and presence of a storybook grandfather. All he needed was an open fire and a pipe to complete the picture. Originally from England, I discovered only recently that alongside ministry he had a talent for sketching and painting. If he was an artist, he was a humble one.

It is hard to say which was more affecting. Joe's warm, melodic voice, rising and falling with measured expression, or his blue eyes, alight behind his glasses. Perhaps it was neither, but the overall impression he exuded of kindness, the authentic sort that you could actually feel. There was no room for cynicism or suspicion where Joe was concerned. Joe was the real deal.

I recall in those early days, before I became a Christian, sitting in the formal church building when he preached, thinking, if this man *really* believes this, maybe I could too. Joe was someone you could trust.

We met in the church lounge room, and I was always a little nervous walking in, though I wasn't exactly sure why. Perhaps I treated preparation less as a helpful aid and more as a test, like I did so many things in life; one I could fail. What if something was uncovered during the sessions, I thought, something that could stop us getting married? I'd heard snippets of information from friends about what supposedly happened in these sessions. Apparently, you discussed tender, serious topics like finances, and future, and potential children (how many you wanted and when, and what method and style of parenting you would adopt, and who knows what elaborate else). All things, in truth, I'd given very little thought to, though I didn't want to admit this. I was young and in love, and so was my almost-husband, and we wanted to spend our lives together. Wasn't that enough? If it wasn't, I was certainly ready to go in fighting to prove that it was. But as it turned out, we spoke very little about any of these things. Joe laid nothing heavy on us. Perhaps with age came added wisdom. Though he never came out and said it, I got the impression that Joe believed that marriage was always going to be bigger than what could be contained in a booklet or a course.

Joe, I'd heard foggily, somewhere in the blurred line between church general-knowledge and gossip, knew tragedy intimately too. Perhaps this, in part, was what made the light shine so bright behind his eyes. Pain has a way of illuminating, even as it darkens.

For whatever reason, Joe cared.

When he spoke, we listened.

'It's no accident that God brought you two together,' he said, his warm gaze moving between us equally. 'Your two stories are now becoming one, and it's a glorious thing.' He said it with a wide, genuine, infectious smile I couldn't help replicating.

I thought of his words often, after, in that first year of marriage. And beyond. Joe seemed to believe that our union was wholly a good thing, so why couldn't I, too? I loved my husband desperately. And I knew he loved me. But was it enough? We were indeed two bodies now become one, something I'd longed for in our three years of dating, but why then did I feel so suddenly lost and adrift? My husband was unendingly patient, a rock in my ocean, but what if, sooner or later, I dragged him down too?

***

Back then, still in our early twenties, that age when friends are like family, and the line between your separate lives is often very slim, I was used to sharing almost everything with my friends. Growing up together, our lives were almost open books. My girlfriends had followed our dating journey and our engagement with eagerness and empathy. I had followed theirs. Several of them had already gone ahead of me into this new world of marriage, like domestic explorers, shining with their discoveries and journeys, returning with their stories. Why, then, was I suddenly now so reticent, so uncharacteristically quiet, afraid to speak about how I was feeling in this new phase of my own marriage? Was I afraid of the lack of parity in our stories and experiences, or of their judgement, or of my own? Or of something else I couldn't even yet name?

Or was I scared that just by defining our difficulties, by speaking them out loud, they would grow even larger?

Rolling in from the big-card celebration voyage of our marriage and back to normal life felt rocky, like stones beneath our feet. I felt a little like a kid at Christmas who, instead of laughingly ripping into all the wrapping paper, had spent her time frozen at the bottom of the tree. Out of sorts, out of season. When anyone asked us how our honeymoon trip was, a honeymoon that had concluded with an unplanned week-long stay at Mike's grandparents' house in the North Island, I simply said, 'Good,' much like when someone asks how you are on a tough day and you say, 'Fine, thank you,' when you clearly aren't. Not if you were to poke under the thin surface of things. Churches, unfortunately, can be infamous for such forms of rehearsed, restrained social behaviour. While no-one would argue it was gospel, cheerful politeness is the general tenor within most church buildings. Forget cleanliness; upbeat smiliness is almost an unofficial mark of godliness, especially among the young, eager, and evangelical.

How could I begin to explain my struggle at this significant crossroads of my life? How could I tell the truth when I couldn't even understand it myself? I adored my new husband; nothing had changed there. He was, in so many ways, my dream come true. Why then didn't I feel dreamier, or at least less nightmarish? For anxiety in many ways had turned even my days into a landscape of fearful unreality. It didn't help that shame kept me from voicing most of what I was thinking, which in turn only increased my personal hall-of-mirrors effect.

In those early years of our marriage, there were secrets I was far too embarrassed to tell anyone. Secrets that I kept hidden behind the closed door of our apartment.

Like how I couldn't fall asleep at night unless my husband was next to me, holding me close.

Like how, when he went out at night to earn some extra money playing guitar in a wedding band, a time he looked forward to and enjoyed, I'd cling to him like a child to their mother on the first day of school, sobbing, so scared of the moment he would drive away, out of view. Only, I wasn't a child, I was a grown adult, a wife. I shouldn't be behaving like this. I was sure none of the other band members had to cope with such preperformance pressure. Such drama.

Like how each time he so much as got into a car and drove off without me, I'd break into a sweat until I knew that he was safe.

I didn't stop to ask why I was feeling like this or to think that maybe it wasn't all my fault, that our bodies have histories too, and that sometimes that history comes with us, into the present. I didn't even know what it was that I was most afraid of: that something would happen to my husband after I said goodbye, after he disappeared into the inky approach of night; or that when the apartment was quiet and still and the darkness descended, anxiety, in the particular hulking guise of PD, would find me again. Again. And I'd cower, defenceless, in its presence. That the walls would close in, and the world would shrink to the size of a pin and take me with it.

Perhaps, most of all, I was afraid I would disappear.

Or that he would.

Or that both of us would.

I was afraid of everything, and I was even afraid of nothing.

More often than not, I was nothing but afraid.

Mike tried his hardest to support me through this early deep valley. He listened, he reassured, he held me as I cried, he rang me from fancy city wedding venues to check in between hasty bites of food, when he should have been enjoying his free gourmet meal in the company of his friends. He loved me, but it was clear he couldn't be my Mr Fixit husband. This wasn't a broken fuse that needed checking—this was a whole, emotional ecosystem that was flickering and faulting. Painful as it was so early in our marriage to admit our overwhelm, it was soon clear that we were facing something bigger than we were able to cope with alone or even together.

It was time to ask for help.

PART III: SURFACING

I just don't want the years to pass
    my life a wrecked vessel adrift and afar,
it'd just be nice to stand up straight—
And 'though the space between ourselves sometimes,
Is more than the distance between the stars'
I think that some friends sitting by my lake in
                                      the afternoon breeze
might sense something of why this place
is an ease for my cares

                                                      —GVDK

Chapter Eleven

The Wise Woman by the Water

The first time I met with my new psychologist, the one who would help me start to turn my life around, I prepared by trying on half the contents of my wardrobe. If a stranger was about to examine me from the inside out, to decode my head and monitor the erratic mood of my heart, I at least wanted to look good while she did it. Perhaps I thought if I could conjure up just the right image on the outside—relaxed, but not too relaxed; put together, without looking overly-calculated; attractive, in a way that suggested I cared about my imprint on the eyes of the world, but not *too* much—she would not startle so visibly when she peeked a little deeper. This time no-one was persuading me into a car to visit a counsellor; I was willingly taking myself to a professional emotional excavator.

What I was most afraid of, of course, was what she would find once she started digging. I was scared of being exposed as the carrier of incriminating internal evidence, evidence so terrible, so far gone that it marked me as unfixable. As permanently broken. Then what?

In hindsight, of course, I can see that I wasn't so much thinking clearly as catastrophising. Exhibiting a classic all-or-nothing mindset. Fusing with my negative thoughts and seeing nothing beyond them. All very common, garden variety anxiety behaviours, if not a bit overgrown in my case. Only I didn't know anything about any of this yet. I didn't realise as I redid my hair for the third time, smoothing down the perennially stubborn waves, that I was about to embark on a years-long education into the mechanics of the mind.

And that, in fact, it *needed* to get messy, that it was necessary to stir up some dirt, before it could start to get better.

***

The Wise Woman by the water, as I came to think of her, had been recommended to us as not just an excellent clinical counsellor, but also a fellow believer. In our earliest days of exploring this crossroads of faith and psychology, we didn't yet know how rare and precious a commodity the union of these two areas were, and how often we too, in the future, would be recommending she and her colleagues to friends, and friends of friends, similarly looking for a high degree of professionalism yoked with a shared faith vision. The Wise Woman occupied an office with several other Christian psychologists near the beaches closest to where we had grown up. Mike drove me there the first time, and many times after, down the winding roads to the coast, the scenery gradually shedding suburbia the further we travelled. That first sight of ocean, suddenly appearing at the peak of a hill, a deep block of solid blue rising to meet the sky, was like a threshold, a ceremonial greeting.

The Wise Woman's office had no view, but its location, nestled amongst shops and cafes, near enough to the ocean to catch its salty breath, gave it a casual, welcoming feel. Compared to the first psychologist's office I'd trialled—the room attached to the man's kitchen, with its invasive noises and feeling of domestic claustrophobia—this humble beachside location seemed like the 'coasties' themselves, with room to exhale, not afraid to take its shoes off and take it slow. Sand and all.

The young receptionist greeted us with a chilled-out smile and a disarming manner that made it seem more like we were reclining together under a tree looking at the waves than sitting on rigid plastic chairs, waiting to be ushered into a clinical appointment. She chatted to us about her day as she made me a cup of tea, 'Did you say one sugar or two?' sharing freely and openly, breaking any notions of preconceived solemnity or imminent emergency. Above her head, suspended over the desk, was a large, horizontal canvas in soft blue tones, and inscribed across it, these words: 'Come to me all who are weary, and I will give you rest'. It was a paraphrase of Matthew 11:28, the verse that sat above my favourite poem, 'atlas'. The poem I always went to when I wanted a place to hide, to feel heard, to remind myself of my brother, and of Jesus. Could it have been just coincidence that it was here?

Mike said he would go for a walk and come back soon.

The Wise Woman appeared from a back room and came forward to greet me, arm outstretched gently. Petite and soft-voiced, with a pixie haircut and floaty bohemian skirt, I was drawn to her immediately. I shook her small, cool hand, aware of the layer of perspiration covering my own. I wondered if she could already sense it in my touch, see it in my eyes: the simultaneous fear of coming apart and the desperate longing for relief.

At first, as I took my place on the sinky-soft couch, grasping a throw pillow to my lap and eagerly accepting the glass of water placed before me, the Wise Woman simply asked questions. She began with the broad and general, 'So, what's been going on lately? What brings you here?' and slowly narrowed down from there, like a series of gentle circles. I had worried about what I would say, how I would explain myself—what if I said the wrong thing? I hadn't known that a good psychologist was like a good director, cajoling words and emotions out into the open and into their places. The Wise Woman spoke rarely, simply listening as I attempted to spill the contents of my interior world, nervously twirling my earring in one hand as I went (a habit I recall having done nowhere else since, but always did there). Despite the nerves, I felt the words coming, flowing forward in a way they hadn't moved on that first problematic visit to a counsellor, or on several other aborted attempts to find someone since. She was interested in my current state, in my feelings of imminent catastrophe, in the claustrophobia-inducing companionship of panic that followed me everywhere, but also in my past. As if it was natural, I told her about Greg, slipping in and out of 'is' and 'was' as I struggled to describe him in all his fullness, in all his searing, baffling absence, as I was to continue to do for many years after.

'I guess the hardest bit of all,' I said into the quiet cocoon of the therapy room, as I took a sip of water and pulled the pillow closer, 'is how afraid I feel now. Ever since my brother died, it's as if the world is no longer what it used to be. It isn't predictable. I just don't feel like it's safe anymore.'

The Wise Woman didn't speak immediately but left a few beats. I wondered in the silence if this was a tactic all counsellors used, if they learnt it in therapy school, to never jump into the gaps too quickly without first giving them time to linger and stretch, further and further, until it felt like anymore tension might cause something to snap. Then they jumped in, like a triumphant, theory-wielding rescuer, with the proper answer. I waited for the punchline, for the correction. But when she did make a reply, it wasn't what I expected.

'You're right.'

All along I'd believed that in coming here it was so I could be rebuffed, redirected, cured of my wrong thinking. Realigned to the positive path of trust and faith. The Wise Woman was a Christian too, she'd help me lean back into my old feeling of security, to defeat and banish fear, to learn to live on the earth again with strong, buoyant steps.

Instead, she agreed with me. 'That's because this world isn't safe,' she continued. 'Not entirely. Not always. Though it might not feel like it, you are seeing the world in more clarity than most people right now.' She paused again and leaned forward. 'And though it doesn't feel nice to realise this, it can actually be a place of deep insight. Of illumination.'

Jesus' words echoed in my mind. Blessed are those who mourn, for they will be comforted (Mt 5:4).

In a way, I suppose, what the Wise Woman gave me in that first session and those that followed, was permission to be afraid. Permission to feel what I was feeling without second guessing it or correcting it constantly, like some sort of emotional editor. Trusting God didn't need to equal a life of undiluted optimism.

Believing in God's protection didn't discount the presence of fear and pain.

God didn't want us to lean into our illusions of security, he only wanted us to lean into him.

Together with the Wise Woman and Mike, who often attended appointments with me, quietly listening, learning alongside me about the intricate nature of the body-mind connection and about how to support the particularly complex inner workings of his wife, I embarked on a new journey that day. Though I couldn't change the way the world turned—so often senseless, cruel, painful—and though I couldn't ultimately change my make-up, my unique individual quirks and frailties, I could change the way I thought about myself in the world and, most importantly, how I thought about God.

After the sessions, Mike and I would walk to the edge of the water together and face out into the vastness of the waves. It became a ritual, almost like a segment of the appointment itself. The movement of the wind on the water echoed the changes that were stirring inside me. Counselling didn't constrain me, or shrink me, in any of the ways I feared. If anything, it helped to blow me open.

***

Anxiety is a thief. It stole many things from me over the years. It stole my belief in the possibility of good outcomes and any calm or casualness around goodbyes. It stole, on many occasions, my appetite, and even my unconscious trust in my own breath. And, in perhaps one of the cruellest acts of all, anxiety stole sunset from me.

There's something about sunsets. I know I'm not alone in thinking this. The colour, the texture, the regular rhythm and the unending variety. Sunsets are God's glory in lights. Sunset is the bridge. The breath between. Sunset is the liminal moment, the end of one cycle, the start of another. As day fades into night, sunset is the breath out and the great settling.

At least it was. Before.

When I was a teenager, with wild, capital 'R' Romantic notions, imagining myself a character in the vein of *Anne of Green Gables* or some other literary heroine, I used to follow the first hint of sunset down the road to the patch of park at the end where I would meet up with a group of my local friends. As the boys chased the soccer ball, and we chased the boys, or as I sat and prayed, or as we engraved our names into the sappy trunk of a tree, blissful sunset came wide over the sky, touching the heads of the gumtrees like a blessing. We'd pause to look up, and for a moment, everything—the trials of our school days, the hidden teen struggles and complicated loves we carried in our hearts, the tasks we faced later that night—seemed to disappear under that regal pastel sweep of sky. Sunset silenced us in the best way.

Sunset hour was a form of sanctuary.

Until one day, it wasn't. I never fell out of love with sunset, but I did start to fear it. With anxiety's arrival, many old familiar things became strange. The gentle, pastel pinks and oranges of approaching night now pulsed with a vivid, heavy new intensity that blazed terror inside me.

If anxiety attacks could be predicted, my hour became that late afternoon hour. As day clung tenuously to the tails of evening, my adrenaline kicked in. I felt delicate, vulnerable, and something else I couldn't seem to describe. For some reason, sunset tore me open and spilled me out.

I told the Wise Woman about it in one of our early sessions.

'What time did your brother die?' she asked me.

I'd become used to her offbeat questions, to her unique way of approaching my problems, often apparently from offstage. But this one seemed to come out of the blue.

'They say 11 am,' I answered.

I had imagined it often. Their car driving down the road from the camping ground, perhaps to pick up some groceries, such an ordinary event, and then a curve in the road (the locals said that it had always been perilous, that they'd tried to alert authorities, that others had spun-out too) and a tree, and then…

'I mean, what time did he die for you?' she said. 'When did you find out what had happened?'

'I guess around 7.30 or 8.00 pm.'

I left the therapy room for a moment in my mind as I remembered. It was summer. We'd made the drive to the Bible study meeting through leafy northern suburbs, the southerly breeze just coming in, the shimmer of day's end flickering off the leaves. I remember the darkness just beginning to form, pooling in the corner of the porch, as Matt told me the news, the last slither of light swallowed into night.

The time that taught me, deep in my body—buried in my muscles at the back of my brain, pierced into my heart—that bad things came after sunset.

'In your mind, your brother died just after the sun said goodbye.' She said it out loud. 'And now, you find it hard to feel secure at sunset.'

She was right. Anxiety thrives on feelings of uncertainty, and sunset was, for me, a precarious turning point. Each day's end brought fresh potential. For bad news. For shock. For permanent—irreversible—endings.

Together, as we spoke the fear aloud, we found ways to deal with it. Bit by bit we—I—began to face sunset. Many other hidden fears were dug out and exposed during that time. Logical and illogical, big and small. And gradually, we tunnelled our way back. Day by day, I began again to see the beauty of the sun in its evening gentleness.

Most of our work took place together in the room: breathing exercises, visualisation, CBT—where I learnt to challenge those thought distortions that were making my life harder than it needed to be, my tendency to catastrophise, to future-predict. Together, we opened my fearful thoughts up, one by one, until they stretched the full perimeter of that small room by the beach. We greeted them, acknowledged their presence without trying to fight or flee from them, and planned how to move through them. I was surprised at how much I took to it, quickly losing my fear of being exposed, and finding instead solace in this process of bearing myself, of unravelling the tangle of secret, hidden threads of thought and feeling. Like any big move, when there are so many boxes to unpack, so much baggage to deal with, it would take several years before we were close to finishing unpacking. The mind is more complex than I had ever known. Not everything it tells us is truth. In that small room, as I dislodged the contents of my thought life, light started to find its way in.

The Wise Woman taught me about body chemistry and about adrenaline and exercise and energy. She taught me how to use my mind—always a vivid imagination factory—as a conjurer of comfort as well as fear. 'You're very good at this,' she told me, as she took me to the imaginative landscapes of my past, and we met them together. She guided me to rest in internal spots of my choosing, memories of camps and rivers, the still waters that lay at the heart of my past. She taught me about the value of the gift of air. She took me right back to basics, teaching me how to breathe again. And occasionally she sent me home with work to do on my own.

One of the most memorable pieces of 'homework' I ever did for the Wise Woman outside of office hours was completing a special psychological questionnaire for people of faith called the Attachment to God Inventory.

Anyone who has read this far knows by now I don't like to make mistakes. If I am given a task, particularly one that involves reading and writing, I apply myself to it zealously, wanting to ensure I get the right answers. At first, I approached the Attachment to God Inventory in this same manner. I sat in our small, modern apartment, with the bathroom that was too big and the living room too small (we had moved several times by then), with the sheet of paper the Wise Woman had handed me, took out my pencil and poised to begin. Like many assessments I'd now completed over the years, this one had a series of propositions and a scale of numbers for the degree of your answer. In this case, it was '7' for 'Agree Strongly' and '1' for 'Disagree Strongly'. I was no amateur by now; I knew there was a pattern they were looking for, a 'right' and 'wrong'. I hoped I'd discern the pattern and answer in the right way.

I read the first question and circled a number. And then the next. But I don't think I was even that far down the page before I forgot about trying to get it correct and in the right order. This was no ordinary task. These words seemed to leap off the page, seemed to probe into me in a way that was so intense it startled me. 'I worry a lot about my relationship with God' one line suggested. Did I agree or disagree? And how strongly? Another asked if it 'is uncommon for me to cry when sharing with God'. Was this true? I definitely cried a lot. But did I do it *with* God? In his presence? 'Daily I discuss all my problems and concerns with God.' Was this true? And if it wasn't true, why not? I can't remember what numbers I circled. But it didn't matter. I wasn't so concerned with the answers but with the very content of the questions themselves. They came from a place deeper than a catalogue. As I read, I sank to the floor and started to cry number seven–level tears. While it's hard to explain, I felt something powerful, something beyond me, like God was speaking to me through that most unlikely of forms, the psychological questionnaire. I didn't hear audible words, but an impression, like God was saying, 'I want you to bring all of you to me, even your tears.' I realised how much I hadn't been coming to him, or how I'd only been stepping so close, like a shy kid in the presence of a teacher. Theoretically, of course, I knew that I didn't need to tidy myself up to come to him, but I had still been feeling, and in many ways acting, like I did. Years later, I would read about the psalms of lament in a helpful book that friends of ours at Bible college put together, and how God wants us in our entirety, even our anger and questions and unedited, bare-faced sorrows. I prayed out loud, sobbing, as I sat with that survey, and I listened to music that reminded me of God's nearness, and in some way, I felt God reaching out to me, calling me without judgement:

'Come.'

'Come to me, all you that are weary and are carrying heavy burdens, and I will give you rest' (Mt 11:28). It was just like the painting over the chilled-out receptionist's head had proclaimed. Like the verse above my brother's poem, the one called 'atlas', which was about looking for a way through to peace.

I'm not sure what the Inventory said about me, but I received a form of answer that day. I woke up to the fact that my emotions, even—especially—my messy ones, mattered to God. He wanted all of me, even my tears. No matter how many or how heavy they fell, he was ready to catch them.

I'd approached counselling like it was the last step before the end, like I might fall over the edge, and I wouldn't ever know how to return. In fact, it was the opposite. I saw and felt firsthand in that humble room, and at home in moments like these, the power in constructive listening, in subtle question asking and, most of all, the comfort in truthful abandonment. As we spoke more, harnessing words and the imagination for good, I felt a little like I was coming back to myself, like the waves were breaking and returning to the soft, warm sand of the shore. In the unveiling, I felt not more naked, but more known. Not more exposed, but more deeply embraced.

Chapter Twelve

Escalators, Aeroplanes, and Stepping-Stone Prayers

To the uninitiated, sitting on a therapist's couch talking about your life might sound easy, perhaps even restful. Maybe we should blame Hollywood for all those depictions of people reclining on velvet chaises with their eyes closed, while their wealthy, well-dressed doctors wait sagely in the corner for them to speak. But in actuality, exploring the depths of one's thoughts, and past, while simultaneously trying to forge a way forward into the future, is rarely straightforward for either client or counsellor.

If therapy brings release, which I found to be true, it is not without work. Sometimes my work with the Wise Woman was wide and panoramic, and sometimes it was narrow and gritty. Sometimes we focused on sunsets, and sometimes our eyes were on the ground.

Sometimes, it was literally about taking the next step. Like the time I had to learn again to ride escalators.

That's right, I am afraid of escalators. Once upon a time, I was terrified of them.

FIGHT, FLIGHT AND FAITH

If I'm looking for a reason to explain it, there was the time I was visiting the UK as part of my gap year adventure the year before my brother died. My mum and grandma had flown over to meet me, three girls on an intergenerational adventure, in a world before September 11, before COVID, before I knew yet to fear fear. We were in the London Underground, Mum and I, travelling down the longest escalator known to man (or, at least until that point, to me); it must have been storeys long. I don't remember feeling any alarm at the size then, even as the businesspeople in heels and long black trench coats sped down the fast lane on important business urgent enough to necessitate running down something designed to rest your legs. We pressed ourselves close to the other side, the tourist side, clutching our shopping bags and, through some fluke of timing, were in just the right place and position to witness a multiple pedestrian pile up at the bottom of the steel stairs. The domino effect created a topple of falling bodies, like the crumpled contents of a fancy, executive walk-in closest. I can't remember if anyone got seriously hurt. I have fragments of memory of a child being carried off, out of the way. It only took less than a minute, perhaps, for the mishap to happen and to be cleared, for us to step freely off at the bottom and move on, but the image stuck in the back of my mind. That time I saw humanity suddenly and helplessly tumble like a set of bowling pins.

Perhaps this is why for years to come, I dreamt about escalators. Long, long escalators, sometimes reaching all the way up to the clouds like Babel's tower. In my dreams, I inevitably lost my grip on the rail, my foot faltered, and I fell; down, down, down to earth. It's the sort of dream that would run on repeat for me. Why?

Perhaps it's because I wasn't just afraid of escalators, I was afraid of losing my footing. I was afraid that one day I'd lose my grip entirely and find there was nowhere safe to land.

I was afraid, ultimately, that there would be nothing, no-one there to break my fall.

***

Several years after I saw the Wise Woman for the first time, I returned for another set of sessions, this time to target a very specific manifestation of my anxiety, not generalised anxiety, but a particular fear that was getting in the way of functioning and that was firing up PD's engines again.

I had become terrified of getting on an aeroplane.

I hadn't always been so stubbornly land-logged, so trembly-winged. Once upon a time—I can clearly remember it—shiny suspended cylinders that bounced and jittered through clouds, equipped with safety vests and whistles and evacuation shoots that looked like slippery dips (*Make sure you remove your shoes first!* they warned in the regulation instructional video played at take-off, as if this would matter), were no undue obstacle for me.

But anxiety can be a leech, an insidious, blood hungry one that is constantly finding new targets to attach itself to, often inexplicably. Or, if you'd prefer a geographical metaphor, it can be a coloniser. It likes to take on new territory. Just when you think you've got a handle on one area, another area of challenge pops up, a leering jack-in-the-box jealous of your attention, 'Hey, look at me!' So it was, after years and years of flying with no problems, my passport enviably full—Europe, China, Fiji, New Zealand, Canada—about six years after that first trip solo to Europe, the leech anxiety met me mid-air in another journey, one I took with Mike and my parents to introduce my new husband to my family overseas. I could blame all sorts of factors for my nerves' mid-air collision: the motel room above a nightclub we stayed in the night before a flight that sent techno pounding through the thin walls and into my bloodstream; the fact that I 'lost' Mike in the airport and we almost missed boarding a flight to Ireland; or, the most likely culprit, the stomach bug I developed on the trip home that saw me hunkered over and helpless for twenty or so hours, just waiting for the end. In a sense, though, the origins are insignificant, because by the time I was twenty-five, I'd developed a full-blown phobia of flying. Just at the time when I needed to return to the sky.

As part of Mike's study, he had scheduled a research trip to the US, a library tour that encompassed the regal book-lined corridors of Yale, Harvard, and Princeton, to name a few. I was determined to go with him; we'd even made plans for me to attend as his official research assistant. Only there was one problem. I was scared to step across the threshold between land and air, onto the magical vehicle of the sky that would take me there.

And, unfortunately, there was no other option.

***

It was the Wise Woman who first taught me the value of step-laddering and 'exposure', of approaching my fears gradually, like a game of 'What's the Time, Mr Wolf?', moving ever so carefully closer towards them until they no longer had the power to chase me away. To catch me.

Exposure was effective, but it wasn't easy. It took hard, and what often felt like humiliating, work.

'We need to find ways to mimic the fear you feel when you step on a plane,' the Wise Woman said. 'Something else similar that you are afraid of, so that we can build up bit by bit.'

She held my faltering gaze in her steady one, waiting for me to say something. But this time she was asking too much. She wanted me to willingly feel the same sort of unsteady terror I experienced when I stepped on a plane? Forgive me if my enthusiasm at helping her out wasn't great.

'What about escalators?' Mike suggested from his seat on the couch beside me. He was sitting in on these sessions, keen to help in any way he could to gently move me forward.

I could have kicked him.

The Wise Woman nodded and took a piece of paper from her desk. She started drawing something, a diagram. 'We need to step-ladder this, so, we will start with a small escalator, perhaps, holding on to the handrail, and then we will go up from there.'

'But why?' I half whined, half protested. I wasn't going down, or up as the case may be, without a fight.

'You need to feel the fear rise and then see what happens next.'

See what happens next? Was she the crazy one now? I'd heard that many medical professionals actually harboured their own secret pathologies.

'The fear will diminish when you don't fight it or try to escape from it. The key is to accept it. What can it really do to you?' I wasn't sure if the question was intended to be rhetorical or not, but I answered it anyway.

'I could fall.'

'But could you, would you? Really?'

'Well, I feel like I will, my hands and legs shake when I panic, what if I—'

'Try it out,' she said. 'Remember, you don't have to love it, you just have to learn to tolerate it. To know it can't really hurt you.'

Even though it feels like it can, I said to myself, even though it hurts like hell, inside.

The idea was not to try to escape, or to even pummel it down (I preferred that idea) but to just let it be. The idea was acceptance. In the face of my greatest enemy, it sounded a little too pacifist for me.

But I wanted to get on that plane, so I agreed to try.

FIGHT, FLIGHT AND FAITH

The first time I 'rehearsed' facing my fear in earnest, we went to a nearby shopping centre with a movie theatre and one of the longest escalators we knew of.

I stood at the top of the metal beast, my legs and hands shaking like I was in the North Pole, while my husband waited at the bottom, a parent at the base of a toddler's slippery dip. I watched all the other people casually riding up and down, seemingly ignorant of the fact they were ascending and descending into imminent catastrophe. Below, Mike beckoned me, like a mere ant in the distance, to just take the first step. Except I couldn't. The shaking had turned me frozen. No matter how much I willed my feet, they wouldn't move. Eventually Mike rode up to find me, and we decided he would step on first, and I would follow. At least that way he'd be in front of me, blocking my view down. Feeling nauseous, I watched him take the first step. I thought of the plane, I thought of how strange I must look to everyone around me, I took a deep breath, and I was on.

I felt the fear and the trembling, the sensation that any moment my knees would buckle, and I'd be gone, a helpless ball of human rolling and bouncing down the steps. I felt the panic rise, hot and powerful, like flames. I felt the pain in the centre of my gut. But nothing further happened. I was okay. I didn't fall. I just got off.

The following week we reported back to the Wise Woman.

'Good,' she said, her face lighting up way more than one would expect someone's face would light up when talking about riding an escalator. 'See. You did it. You stood with the panic. You didn't run.'

'But it hurt.' Anxiety hurts, like, physically. People don't tell you that.

'But what did it do to you?' she said, as if she could hear my thoughts. 'Did it stop you reaching your destination?'

'No, but it's an escalator, it takes less than a couple of minutes. A plane trip, especially across the world, takes hours.'

'We are getting there,' she assured me in her infuriatingly calm way. 'You *will* get on that plane, trust me.'

***

Alongside the practices of step-laddering and exposure, another practice grew within me during this time, quietly and surely. I started praying what I now call 'stepping-stone prayers'. Not the big, desperate, please-heal-me-now-once-and-for-all-totally-and-completely type of prayers, but much humbler, grassroots, moment-to-moment requests. Small, solid, place-able prayers, like stepping stones across a river, enough to feel the support beneath my feet, to know that there is a way forward—not around, but through—one step at a time. The types of prayers that recognised that God was with me, not just if the anxiety disappeared but *in* the very heartbeat of pulsing anxiety, pulling me through. The type of prayers that recognised that just because God didn't take my panic away, it didn't mean that he went away as well. That believed that if I squinted, I could still glimpse God's watchful presence even in the eye of the panic.

I remember praying for stepping stones on each plane ride: the practise one the Wise Woman made me undertake interstate to prepare, and the real overseas one.

Perhaps God knew that what I needed most of all during these times was something outside of myself to draw me out, to distract me, to divert me from my panic, and ultimately to redirect me. Perhaps that's why he always sent me seats next to the most interesting of fellow passengers.

I met Ted for the first and only time on a ninety-minute interstate flight. Ted was a small, elderly man, ordinary looking to the point of invisibility in any other scenario. I'm pretty certain I never would have spoken to him, had he not been squished awkwardly in the row of three seats beside me and my husband, if he hadn't opened his mouth to speak to the pale, deep breathing, chewing-gum chewing, water sipping, crossword-completing woman beside him.

'Are you coming or going?' he asked.

'Going,' I replied, shakily. I didn't feel like I had many words to offer. 'And you?'

'I'm returning home,' he said, a tinge of pride in his gruff voice. He turned to look at me more closely, his crinkled-at-the-corner blue eyes lighting up. 'I just completed a weekend at a stutterer's convention.'

'Oh,' his words were surprising enough to cause me to forget my racing heartbeat for at least a beat.

He needed no more encouragement to continue. 'All my life I've had the most terrible impediment, it's prevented me from doing so much, you know. I thought I'd never find anywhere I fit in. And then I joined this group, and it's been helping, it helped me face my fears, you know?'

Was he asking if I knew anything about facing fear? It was almost too funny to take in. 'That's great,' I replied simply. I couldn't actually hear his stutter. I think I said this, told him how it must have helped.

'I'm not nervous right now,' he said. 'It happens more in public, you know, like when I have to talk to groups. In fact,' he shifted in his chair, 'I have one last task to do, to complete the weekend's work. I better go and get started.' He stood, slowly, unravelling his seatbelt from the airline supplied headphones, unfolding his body in an awkward, jerky manner.

'You have a task to do. Here?'

'Yes,' he replied, as if it was self-evident. 'I've been told I need to go to the front of the plane and give a speech over the loudspeaker.'

I had, by this time, forgotten my own fear. But I could see signs of the fear growing in him. And something else. A sort of unhinged, liberated, just-north-of-normal confidence.

I watched him make his way unsteadily to the front of the plane. If I'm honest, I prepared to cringe a little. I'd only known him a few minutes, in the strangely intimate setting of the plane, but I felt already a sort of protective ownership of him. What if he embarrassed himself? He almost certainly would. He was almost childishly naive, hopeful. I doubted they'd even let him speak.

He was gone for quite some time. Close to landing, a message came over the loudspeaker. 'This is your captain speaking. Soon we will begin our descent, but first we have a special guest. Please make him welcome.'

My new friend came on to the speaker. I now heard his stutter, clearly exposed, as he began, as he openly and vulnerably explained where he had been and the purpose of what he was doing. There was no poetry to what he said, no puns even, the content was honest and open, like him. He made it through his whole speech, concluding with words of gratefulness to us, his fellow passengers, for allowing him to speak.

For a moment, silence followed. I swallowed hard. And then the whole plane erupted into cheers and clapping. I brought my own hands together after I brushed at a few stray tears.

'I did it!' he said on returning, a beaming smile illuminating his humble face.

The plane began its descent, and I chewed more gum to stop my ears from popping. I braced, as I always did, for the impact. We said goodbye as we gathered our bags from the overhead lockers. We might have awkwardly hugged. I watched his small, slow figure merge into the crowded line.

Perhaps to anyone else's eyes this was not a stepping stone at all, just a quirky tale of coincidence, a moment of levity in the sky. But to me it was even more than a stone, it was a sign. Aren't we, in the end, all just stutterers trying to make our way home?

Wherever in the world did we get the idea we had to walk through life unafraid or we couldn't walk at all? Walking scared might look like hands shaking, stomach lurching, knees knocking (though I'm not sure my knees have ever actually really knocked), words stopping and stumbling, but it's better than pretending we are invincible or that we can do it all effortlessly. And it's better, too, than believing fear has the final answer, the last push, the freefall without a parachute.

In the end, we made it to New York, to the land of libraries, and bagels, and miles-long bookshops, on a wing and a whole host of small, but vital, stepping-stone prayers. I felt the fear, and I waited, and it passed.

Anxiety and I were in the sky together, and for a moment, we were flying.

Chapter Thirteen

Anxiety and Its Allies

One of anxiety's most dubious superpowers is its ability to isolate, to make the world shrink, and you within it, until you feel completely alone. A fragment of an island, far from the mainland. Despite this fact, anxiety hardly ever journeys unaccompanied. It is rarely, if ever, a standalone issue. Like other mental illnesses, anxiety has its co-conditions, its companions, its allies in upheaval, and they can and do very often work together, brushing up against one another, colliding, colluding, and exacerbating each other's effects.

As I'd learnt from my time with the Wise Woman, we are intricately interconnected beings; sometimes our minds affect our bodies, and sometimes our bodies affect our minds. And more often than not, the two dance together until it can be hard to distinguish who is leading and who is following. Anxiety is mental, and it is physical. It is found in the head and the heart and the impressionable rim of the lower back. For this reason, it can often feel all-encompassing. Perhaps this is why we anxiety sufferers so often want to flee. We don't just want to leave a certain place, we want to run until we can escape our very own shells, our very own selves.

FIGHT, FLIGHT AND FAITH

For me, and I do not think this is unusual, anxiety has most often linked arms with the deepest, most sensitive parts of me: my guts, my stomach, my tender midsection. They don't call the gut the second brain for nothing. If, for some reason, my stomach was upset, it was almost certain to spread the message to my mind, and sooner or later, my whole self would be at sea again.

***

From babyhood, I had a rare skin disease called urticaria pigmentosa. Red, inflamed hives wrapped my torso all the way up to my neck, sparing only my face. Children at school sometimes called me Chicken Pox, and my mum was asked on numerous occasions if what I had was catching. It wasn't. But it was painful. Not only did it manifest in itchy, external spots, made worse by the humid Sydney weather, it played internally with my stomach due to excess acid. To deal with my condition, I regularly visited the child health centre with my mother to see an older doctor with cold hands and a kind, solemn way of speaking. While he examined me, pressing down on the soft skin of my stomach, I would look up into his face, at his high, serious forehead, where I assumed he stored all his grand knowledge, and at the strange rim of grey hair at the edges, like that of an elderly, melancholy clown. There was only one redeeming part of these trips. The serious doctor had a large mural on his office wall, chock-full of fairytale characters. It was as if every children's book that had ever been written had a representative there, all playing happily together under the wide, bright arc of a rainbow. I remember focusing on that mural during the examinations, wanting to be any one of those jovial characters, away from this place of illness. In another body that didn't need to be poked and prodded and medicated.

As a kid, I managed my stomach problems with the prescribed meds, ordinary painkillers, and a liberal dosage of lemonade. Flat or fizzy, it didn't matter, both seemed to work, especially on long car trips when the nausea was strong. Mercifully, my childhood illness had an expiration date. By the time I was a teenager, by the time I stepped over the threshold of that awkwardly-named life stage, 'puberty', the doctor and my parents reassured me, the spots, and hopefully the pain too, would leave me. As such, I looked forward to it eagerly, eschewing the embarrassment that seemed inevitable for the relief it would bring. But then something else arrived, earlier and with far more intensity than expected.

***

I sat on the cold, hard floor of the kitchen while my mum did the after-dinner dishes. The cramps were lower down in my abdomen than I was used to, spreading even to the base of my thighs, and different in intensity and sensation somehow to my normal stomach pain. I bent over with my arms pressed into my waist, trying to relieve the ache with pressure. When the cramps still didn't go away later that night, I lay in my parents' bed, cradling a hot water bottle, pressed between them like I'd done as a much smaller child, and counted the waves of pain, audibly, as they continued through the night. I slept sparingly, as I'm sure my parents did too, and only in the morning did I wake to the shock of an answer.

'Your period.' My mum affirmed what I already suspected from the awkward body education classes we'd been made to do at our small primary school. I could see she was a little surprised herself at the expediency of the arrival. I was barely twelve years old. I didn't start grade seven until the following year. Womanhood had collided head-on with childhood, and I was given no choice in the matter. Suddenly, without my permission, I was thrust into a new, complex world of feminine hygiene products and anti-inflammatory pills. As a way of coping, perhaps, with all the dimensions of the change, I took it upon myself to become a detective, watching my friends for signs of their own unexpected arrival, asking subtle, or not so subtle, questions, to try and see if anyone else was ready to join me on this new road. But despite my attempts at finding companionship, it seemed I was alone. My best friend didn't get her own welcome to womanhood event until a couple of years later, by which time I'd filled her in on most of the awkward details. And, as far as I know, none of my girlfriends experienced anything close to the level of discomfort I had.

By the time I was around fourteen and had spent several years with not only the pain but also unusually heavy and longstanding bleeding, my mum made a decision. She took me to a specialist in women's issues, rightly concerned that what was happening each month in her daughter's body was something beyond the bounds of normal.

'It's just hormones, an adjustment phase,' the female specialist said as I lay with my tender teenage belly exposed, self-conscious and cold on her examination table, feeling far worse than I ever had when I was under examination by the serious doctor of my childhood. There was no mural to distract me, and even if there had been, surely I was too old for fairytales. 'She'll grow out of it in a few years,' the specialist decreed, her words colder than her fingers. We were sent away curtly, dismissed, with no more information or help than when we walked in.

Only I didn't grow out of it, it only grew worse.

The pain in my belly radiated through not just my body, but my life.

And along with it, subtle messages found their way into my fragile, still-forming sense of self. If there was nothing there, after all, beyond what everyone else experienced, then why did I feel like this? If a doctor hadn't been able to find anything that was actually wrong with me, maybe it wasn't there. But what was left then? I think it was about this time that I began to see myself as in a slightly different category to my more robust peers: a little more fragile, a little less able to cope. If my physiology wasn't the problem, then maybe I was?

***

I didn't find out I had endometriosis, or its cute little nickname, endo (used by those in the know—and it didn't seem like too many people were, or at least they hadn't been until very recently), until I was twenty-seven years old and had been married for over three years. By this time, endo had been hanging out inside me, secretly, for well over a decade, like a cocky criminal convinced it would never get caught, spreading not only physical disease but a lack of mental ease too. Endometriosis, it appears, is vastly undiagnosed, and diagnosis most often only takes place after many, many years of suffering. My story, sadly, was only a drop in the ocean of similar stories of pain. In the end my stowaway endo only came out of hiding because of another new, important, bodily obstacle. No matter how hard we tried, it seemed we couldn't convince my body to accommodate a new life.

***

I still remember the moment I found out the news I'd been waiting all week for. I was in the upstairs storeroom of the quaint little bookshop I worked in at the time, a labyrinthine space stuffed full of boxes of books straight from the warehouse, emanating the inimitable aroma of new page smell. I'd been checking my email on the desk top computer several times an hour when, finally, the message came in. I'd made it! Not only had I secured a place to do my doctorate in creative writing, I'd also won a scholarship to support it.

I ran down the stairs to tell my bosses, a quirky husband-wife partnership who spent half the workday bickering in a way that was only partly affectionate. The husband half of the boss duo congratulated me in a reserved, distracted way. I could already see his brain ticking over with potential staffing concerns. His wife caught more of the current of the mood and enfolded me in a warm, if brief, hug. I appreciated at least her attempt to share my happiness. But neither of the pair were the people I really wanted to tell. News like this needed people who *knew* me, who understood how much work it had taken to get here, how much I wanted this. As if by divine arrangement, at that very moment, my friend Bec spontaneously walked through the door.

Blonde and upbeat, Bec was my get-it-done, positive friend, always there to cheer others on. There couldn't have been a better person to give me the reaction I craved. 'Bec!' I practically bowled her over with my greeting. I didn't stop to question the reason for her suddenly leaving her own workday to visit me then. I saw only the opportunity for my own gratification. 'I'm so glad you're here. I have something I have to tell you.'

She grinned back at me, a glow of what I thought was reflective glee. 'Me too,' she said.

We hardly made it to the walkway out of the front of the store before both our words burst forth, like geysers. 'I got a scholarship to do my PhD. I'm starting next semester,' I announced.

'I'm pregnant, our baby is due in six months,' she bounced back.

'That's amazing!' we both said.

And it was. Why then did my own news seem to pop and fizzle as I stared into the elated blue eyes of my dear soon-to-be-a-mother friend? I was happy for her, of course I was, but I couldn't help feeling something else too, something hard to articulate or explain, or even to name, because it wasn't a something, it was more of a nothing. An absence that ached like a very present pain. Where I'd been full-to-the-brim of my own news only moments before, I suddenly felt very, very empty.

***

In the early years of our marriage, the subject of babies hadn't come up much. Our time and attention were consumed with learning to live together as husband and wife, in making ends meet (or often not) and in focusing on the work of learning to cope with my anxiety with the help of the Wise Woman. Besides this, we weren't the most practical people. I was more of a nerd girl than a maternal girl. As still-in-progress young academics and creatives, we weren't the type to make long-term plans. A family beyond the two of us seemed in the beginning, at least, a way off in the distance. A future we blithely assumed would just fall into place *someday*.

But as we passed the midpoint of our twenties, the future drew a whole lot closer. All around us, our friends were becoming glowing advertisements for pregnancy and parenthood. It's hard to say exactly when, or how, but one day *someday* arrived, and we decided it was our time to try too. Perhaps it was all the hours we had spent with our close friends and their new offspring, getting to know babies as little, distinct people rather than just concepts. Or perhaps there were even deeper reasons, longings I felt needed to be met on a wider level than even us. I was acutely aware that I was, for my mum at least, the only remaining child capable of procreating. No-one else could carry on our family line, nobody else could give her that coveted and knighted title of 'grandmother', a title I was already confident she was made for and would wear and exercise so well. A part of me even dreamt of a little boy, in the image of my brother; not to replace him, of course, but perhaps, maybe, in some small way, to extend a part of him into the future.

And so we started, in the lingo of the time, not-not-trying, and when this very casual, see how it goes, leave it all to God approach yielded no results, we started more actively trying. And after over a year of this approach, with no results, we started asking some tentative questions. And, eventually, when no answers came, we decided to go out and purposefully find some.

From our late twenties, after pouring ourselves into counselling and understanding my mental health, a different, invisible foe entered our lives and moved in for the next five years. The spectre of infertility. The new challenge to not only our physical bodies, but also, of course, our minds and hearts.

***

For every bad professional we encountered on our journey for answers to my body's problems, there was a good one. The doctor who first diagnosed me, and much later became the man who delivered my first two babies, was one of them. From the moment of walking into Dr A's office, we felt a certain confidence. Kindness and calm wisdom, coupled with just the right amount of jovial, doctorly humour (and appropriate humour is important when discussing one's most vulnerable places) characterised his approach as we first encountered him, and has done so consistently since knowing him. A simple examination with his large, capable hands was all that was needed for Dr A to tell us what no-one else had yet been able to. 'I'm almost certain you have endometriosis,' he said.

Naming has power. Especially when the name so perfectly fits the experience. At first, we were elated, which, of course, sounds strange, as we had just received rather serious information, although we didn't yet know the severity of it. But there is something so relieving about being heard, at last, at realising that you didn't imagine it all along, that indeed something was wrong. I wasn't just crazy or hysterical, or overly sensitive, which, by the way, seemed to be terms so often relegated specifically to the realm of women's issues. I was unwell. With the naming came hope. Now that we knew what was wrong, surely we could fix it, right?

Dr A, unfortunately, could do nothing more for us at this stage. He referred us on with the rather monumental words, 'Come back to me when you are pregnant.' A good metaphor to describe infertility is that of a train ride. Not an express train but a protracted, frustrating, all-stops one. This was still just the beginning of our tour. But we had begun.

From Dr A we stopped off next at Dr B. Where Dr A was almost fatherly in his approach, solid and reassuring, Dr B was smooth. Smooth skin, smooth voice, and small, smooth surgeon's hands. His handshake on greeting was soft, barely connecting, and it made me question from the beginning my certainty in this next step. Thankfully, his knowledge seemed superior to his relational skills. The only way to offer a foolproof diagnosis of my endometriosis, he told us, was to examine by keyhole surgery under anaesthetic. At this point our journey became an exploratory mission. And the directions were vague. *If* they found endometriosis in there, they would operate on the spot as they found it. If not, they'd sew me up and on we'd go.

If there is a list of settings anxiety finds particularly distasteful, like a top ten of anxious hotspots with warnings, like *Do not visit here; if you do, take precautions and expect anxiety manifestations,* hospitals would have to be at the top of the list. I went in for day surgery nervy and hungry, my throat dry, and not just from not drinking for so many hours. As they wheeled me along on the hospital bed, I felt my heart whirring faster than the metal wheels, the fluoro overhead lights and overly clean surfaces blurring in some sort of antiseptic nightmare-scape. Thankfully anaesthetic doesn't take its directions from anxiety, or I'm not sure I ever would have got on the table, especially since the anaesthetist assigned to me was a dour man with disappointingly inexpressive eyes, as if his personality had been scrubbed away with everything else. I closed my own and waited.

I woke blurry and confused in the recovery ward, a kind nurse bending over to greet me, her own eyes much warmer, to find the investigation mission had gone well. That is, they found what they were looking for. A whole lot of it. I didn't just have some endometriosis; I housed my own colony. My insides were fused together like glue. My tubes were blocked thick like a smoker's lungs. Even my bowel was affected. On follow-up appointments, Dr B delighted in showing me the gory images, like gruesome holiday snaps taken when I wasn't aware there was a camera in the room. We were undergoing an education in endo. Endo is measured in stages. One is the least vicious case, while four is the worst. I had stage four. Severe. However, it seemed like they had been able to burn most of it out. My sizzled insides and I stayed in hospital for three days that first time. I was bloated like an overblown balloon and feeling shock-shaken. But at least we'd done it. We'd defeated the endo enemy, or so we thought, for now.

At a follow-up appointment with Dr B, we received instructions for yet the next leg of our journey. With the surgery behind us and my system 'clear' for the moment, he suggested the time was nigh for action in the form of further medical assistance to see if we could kickstart those sluggish pregnancy vibes. Short of full in-vitro fertilisation (IVF), which we weren't yet prepared to undertake for various reasons (not the least of which was more intrusive medical intervention), we tried everything Dr B suggested. But it appeared, even after surgery, that everything still wasn't enough.

And so we stepped back on the infertility train, our travel luggage becoming increasingly heavy to carry, our bodies and brains dragging.

Keen not to miss any opportunities though, we tried other, different, more off-the-beaten-track directions in our journey too, including alternative, herbal medicine. We found ourselves in many more waiting rooms. One in particular reminded me distinctly of a set from a Harry Potter movie, with ancient looking bottles and vials lining the shelves like righteous, crusading soldiers. The man who ruled it all spoke at us from behind his large wooden desk, splayed messily with papers (he did not use a computer and I was not sure if this gave him more credibility or less). He told us somewhat dramatic tales of his pioneering work in the area of a particular herb, of where his method had succeeded when so many others hadn't. We were to hear this again and again, promises that this time we were in the right hands. He told us of couples from overseas who had come specifically to seek his aid, how he alone was able to give them the answers they sought. At the end of our first consultation, he handed us two black glass bottles of the foulest, most expensive herbs I have ever held, and told me to drink it before my meals.

'Let's see if this will help you fall,' he said with a wink.

'Fall' was his archaic term for pregnancy, for falling pregnant, and it was the same word he used week after week as we returned to see him, after an hour-long drive, still hopeful. We didn't fall, no matter how carefully I carried those black glass bottles with me in my handbag wherever we went. I worried constantly about breaking them, about forgetting to take them; and when I did remember, I tried not to gag as I drank. After nearly a year of seeing the man with the big promises and grand stories, we decided it was time to move on.

We didn't fall in the way he intended, but we did stumble, falling in hope, in finance, in energy. Sometimes, the longer and harder you try at something, the more you start to lose perspective. As I've been recounting the physical details of this part of our journey, I'm not sure if I've yet managed to convey the degree of ongoing emotional pressure. Any fertility journey, because of its length, its stubborn twists and turns, its deflating dead ends, can be very wearying. We were weary, and we were trying our hardest to make new life. A strange and ironic partnering. One of the key decisions with any fertility journeys is how, exactly, to pace it. Such journeys tend to be long distance, but how long? You don't want to risk running out of steam. And the question is always there: Will it ever end, or, even more sombre, when should *we* end it? All the questions, all the uncertainty, all the weariness, pulled at our already frayed nerves.

And then there were the comments. People began to notice our delayed start. Those close to us, of course, treated the situation with the utmost of discretion and empathy, but there were others who made their own conclusions. No doubt such comments were innocently intended, but this made them no less deeply felt. Anyone who has grappled with infertility will know such responses. *When will we hear the pitter patter of tiny feet?* (By the way, what child ever pitter patters? They thump, and jump, and other far livelier, less sedate terms.) Along with the comments came advice in various degrees of unhelpfulness, ranging from uninformed to highly hurtful. 'Just relax,' we were told by often much older friends and family. 'Your body will do its work when you are calm.' Telling this to an already anxious person, even one who doesn't harbour a long history with GAD and PD, is the equivalent of holding a gun to their head and telling them to just chill out. The art of relaxation itself can become a new pressure, a new burden to bear.

But in truth, the comments weren't any less troubling than what I was already telling myself. While we were definitely on this journey together as a couple, in the end it was my body that was the problem. Me. Perhaps my thoughts as a teenager weren't so far off the mark after all. There was only one conclusion to be made from all of this, as time wore on and on without results. My body was busted. Like a piece of broken machinery. I didn't work. My insides were like glue. I'd seen the gory photos. I'd heard the negative predictions. And like any good perfectionist woman, I began to hear something else too, at first quiet, in the distance and, as time went on, growing closer and persistently louder: the distinct sound of failure bells ringing. I began to blame myself for what was happening—or wasn't happening, in this case.

And alongside the failure narrative, in the hollow created by sadness and struggle and accumulated uncertainty, other old stories, other preworn patterns, began to resurface.

Chapter Fourteen

Running South

I would love to tell you that this is a story that traces a continuous, smooth arc of healing, a well-shaped line of recovery. I long to say that after working so hard and so successfully with the Wise Woman, everything not only got so much better, but it stayed that way. I had learnt how to accept my anxiety, and to not let it boss me. I'd experienced my attachment to God at a deeper level. I'd balanced, for a time, on the solid bottom of stepping-stone prayers. From then on in, it was all herbal tea and extended yoga poses. Of course, I'd love to tell you that that's what happened. To hold my story out to you like a Christmas gift, gorgeously wrapped. And if so, then we could stop here and communally exhale (not a bad idea to do anyway, by the way). But that wouldn't be the whole story. I'd be lying, showing you only half the picture, if I didn't tell you about the years of darkness that followed.

And ultimately, I'd be robbing you of the quality of the light that eventually emerged.

***

I wonder sometimes if it is the invisible obstacles in life, the hidden spaces, that can be the hardest to deal with. The seen things can at least be touched, sized up, accounted for. Shared and aired in the open. But the unseen things live silently inside us, rumbling and writhing and brewing away, often unrelentingly. As with anxiety, infertility isn't always obvious to the naked, or the uneducated, eye. It is called, appropriately, a silent grief, a continual loss of what could have been. But to the one carrying it around, the absence can feel so present, so glaringly visible, that it obscures everything else in its path.

A couple of years into our infertility journey, the mute pressure of our childlessness was building to a roar inside me. I didn't know how much longer I could stay in limbo while other people's good-fertility fortune was paraded in front of me. Our friends were becoming professional family builders, climbing in and out of maternity clothes for the second or even third times. It felt like we were on a racetrack that had markings for everyone else but us. We were continually being lapped. It's not that I begrudged them, or at least I did my best, most of the time, not to. But to say I didn't, even unconsciously, compare myself to my increasingly blooming friends and feel my own lack as an actual ache in the pit of my ever-flat stomach, would be a lie.

My feet weren't just itchy for movement, for escape, for a way out of the baby bubble—they burned.

***

At first when we heard of a possible job opportunity for Mike interstate, we tried not to hang our hopes too heavily upon it. The academic market in Australia is small and crowded. For every available position, there are dozens of eager suitors in hot pursuit, trailing impressive reams of degree-filled resumes behind them. Mike hadn't even finished his PhD yet, and anyone who has done a PhD knows how long and winding and elusive the road to completion can be, filled with endless corrections and the wild goose chase of footnotes. It could be months or even years before he really finished. But when we received news that he had made the selection panel's shortlist, we went out and bought him a new suit, and while Mike caught an early morning flight for the interview round, I stayed behind in Sydney and prayed. Not just mild, casual prayers either, but specific, fervent petitions, asking for this to be God's will —and also willing it to be.

Not even an hour after he completed his interview, barely enough time to strip off his tie and order a cup of coffee, Mike received a phone call. The interview had gone better than he'd thought. The job was his, if he wanted it. In an industry that typically moves at a professorial snail's pace when it comes to decision-making, it was the fastest turnaround we'd ever seen, and it required a quick response from our side too. They wanted to know his answer by the close of day.

'By the close of the day, that's only a few hours away,' I said, unable to keep the excitement from my voice as we hungrily grabbed a few moments to speak before he stepped back onto his flight home.

'We'd be crazy to let this go,' one of us, both of us, said. God had to be in this, we agreed, marshalling evidence in an argument we'd already ruled on.

Mike touched down in Sydney late that afternoon. By evening he had rung them back to accept the position. By that night we were celebrating our fresh-off-the-press news in a cafe. In a cluster of recent losses, this was a win. In a stalemate on the fertility front, this felt like a fresh start. The news appeared solid enough to clutch a hold of and lean forward into. And lean in we did. We would move interstate in less than eight weeks.

If our family had any reservations about the haste of our decision, they kept it to themselves, but our sun-loving Sydney friends were not so quiet. Were we sure that we had thought it through enough, they asked us. It all seemed so sudden. And what about the Melbourne weather. The cold?

'But we love the cold,' we invariably replied. It was true; we both jumped at any opportunity to don a scarf and jacket, to sit by a fireplace, a rarity in milder Sydney. But the truth was, even if we heard their objections, we weren't open to considering them. I, for one, wanted this move more than I dared to explore. And not just because of the promised job security.

We were off on an adventure—or was it an escape? The funny thing about those two words is that they can be much closer than you'd ever think, or like, to admit. If various places we lived were like relationships, Melbourne was our fling, our crazy romance, perhaps even our rebound, when years of infertility in Sydney broke our hearts. And in the beginning, at least, the romance felt very good.

***

'You could argue this city is made for you.' Our friend and former pastor Justin's voice came over the speaker phone in the car as we drove around the streets of Victoria's capital city for the first time. With all the opportunities to drink in art and quality coffee, to browse bookstores, to hear live music, to taste any and every style and type of cuisine, we couldn't agree more.

'It's more like Europe than Australia,' we said to each other, a mini-Europe transplanted into the bottom corner of our big Southern Hemisphere island, complete with trams and seasons that actually changed.

Finding a home in this new, made-for-us city, however, was harder than we'd anticipated. We'd done our research ahead, scouring rental websites, lining up possible suburbs to try in close proximity to Mike's work. But eagerly expectant drive-bys revealed dingy apartments in unattractive streets, with no relational reference points for us. We didn't yet have an idea of a church to attend, we barely knew a soul here outside the people who had hired Mike and a few friends of friends. Melbourne was indeed a blank canvas, but we didn't know where to aim our brush. When one of Mike's new colleagues told us about St Kilda, an artsy, urban suburb that was also positioned beside the water, we were reminded immediately of the areas surrounding USYD back home. This, at least, seemed to make some sense. We decided to give our paintbrush a try on the bayside suburb.

The first St Kilda apartment we inspected was shoe-box tiny and at the back of a complex so beefed up on security that we felt like we had visited a high detention maze. By the time we'd made it through multiple corridors to view what was basically a single room chopped up into tiny, windowless pieces, we began to doubt our friendly informant's sanity. Stepping out again to find a place to have lunch, a photo in a real estate agent's window caught our attention. *Regal two-bedroom beauty in prime position. This one will go quickly*, the advertisement read. Without even asking Mike what he thought, I darted through the door and expressed my desire to see the apartment in the window. The young woman behind the desk must have smelt an easy catch, because barely an hour later we pulled up outside the property with a set of keys.

The two-bedroom art deco apartment with decorative high ceilings and period leadlight details seemed practically palatial in contrast to the previous one. I literally skipped down the long wooden corridor. *This is it!* my overly impulsive gut told me. 'This is the one,' I said out loud to Mike, before we'd even made it back into our car, pinning him into an emotional corner tighter than the bathroom in the last apartment.

Another couple walked through just after us, making approving noises to one another as they tilted their heads to examine the cornices. I could already picture them mentally arranging their furniture in front of the quaint, decorative fireplace in the living room, making their meals in the intimate kitchen. We needed to get our game faces on if we wanted to win this. With a few pressured phone calls and pens to the grindstone, we had the forms to apply for the apartment filled out by later that afternoon. At 5 pm, as we were getting back into our car again, we received the phone call to say it was ours for the renting.

That night we were scheduled to have dinner at the home of relatives of Emma's husband, a family we had met briefly over the years at birthday parties and weddings and other celebrations. We were tired, but still very keen to make contact with any familiar faces in this new place. We drove the distance from the congested inner city to the outer suburbs, watching the view from the car windows stretch to incorporate more green space the further we travelled. On arrival, the family welcomed us warmly into their cosy home. We ate a lovely, conversationally-rich dinner out on their patio, the night air fresh but my head spinning from the exhaustion of the day.

'I can't believe you found a place already,' Em's sister-in-law, Kris, said. 'We know another couple who took weeks to find somewhere that fit all their criteria.'

For the first time, as I took in her words through the haze of my fatigue, I felt a twinge of unease. Was it possible that we had been too quick to make our decision? Had we really stopped to think about all the pros and cons and weighed them against one another, or had we only seen what we wanted to see in the moment?

The first few months of our new life in St Kilda passed in a pleasant if not steamy blur, seeming to confirm us in our decision. We lost ourselves in the enchantment of a Melbourne summer, in the forgetfulness of a new culture and space. During the day hours we worked, Mike in his new, demanding role of lecturer in American history to over two hundred first year students, while simultaneously juggling the final stages of his thesis, me on my dissertation and novel-in-progress in the library or cafes around his office. But the evenings were for leaving the books behind and exploring. Our apartment was in easy walking distance to the water, and we often wandered down to the long pier and followed the wooden planks to the very end point where a colony of tiny penguins regularly visited. I loved to watch their quaint comings and goings or to listen to the varied accents and banter of the regular fishermen who gathered there. More often than not, we ate out in the many lively restaurants and cafes of our new multicultural suburb. Pizza, the best we had ever tasted, the dough rolled and flipped on the spot; Mexican, made from scratch and out-of-this-world good; and vegetarian and vegan options galore. Our wallets opened, and our tastebuds took their fill.

'We should really go home,' we'd turn and say unconvincingly to each other over and over again. Invariably we would still be there long after the sun dipped its body into the water in a solid orange ball to the tune of backpacking bongo players and fire-twirling revellers.

In the beginning of our stay, we welcomed the noise, the texture, the action. Luna Park with its kitsch and colourful history, its constant in-the-moment movement, and the chaotic charm of the night markets, a cacophony of languages at every corner, so different from the staid, quiet suburbs of our upbringing, the cul-de-sac of homogeneity we had come from.

That first summer we managed to leave the unresolved issue of our ability/inability to have children mostly unopened, buried deep in our boxes under other more immediate, pressing concerns. But by autumn, we had no other choice but to unwrap it and face it once more.

***

A month or so prior to moving to Melbourne, on New Year's Eve, we'd spent the night in the New South Wales Snowy Mountains, just the two of us, doing something we had never done before. Rather than joining friends for a party, or even spending the night in front of the TV watching the year in review and the mediocre pre-fireworks commentary, we devoted the entire evening to prayer: for an answer, for a resolution, for some sort of movement forward on the fertility front. We prayed long and hard and in great detail. We prayed on our knees and from the bottom of ourselves. We laid it all out on the carpeted patch of floor in a small apartment overlooking the lake, with the mountains in the distance, so far from our new home.

And then, as the excitement of the new year faded, we came back down from the mountains to ground level once more, to the ordinary, concrete, immediate tasks before us: packing up an entire apartment and following a moving truck through the night and over the border south. If I'm honest, I'm not sure if, beyond that night of the year's switching, we even expected anything in return, despite the fact we'd gone to such effort to ask. We had become so accustomed to searching for results that the act of searching itself had become almost like a destination.

But then, in the middle of our scuttling and packing and preparing, something unexpected happened. Just weeks away from our move, my mum approached us, tentatively, with some new information.

'I know it's terrible timing,' she circled in cautiously. 'But I thought you might want to know something.' We waved her hurriedly on. My mother is a marvellous storyteller. Even her preamble can be pages long. We wanted to know the punchline.

It turned out that one of my mum's friends had a daughter who had recently given birth. Her friend's daughter had endometriosis. Her friend's daughter had seen and been treated by an exceptional doctor. Had we heard of him? No. We'd never heard of him, which was somewhat strange as we soon found out that he was famous (perhaps infamous is a more accurate term) in endometriosis treatment circles.

'Would you be interested in seeing him?' Mum asked. If so, she had taken down his number and could give it to us.

She was right. It was terrible timing. But then again, it couldn't hurt, we supposed, to just go one time and see. Could it?

***

With only a couple of weeks to go before our interstate move, we successfully landed our first appointment with Dr C, or Dr god, small 'g', as we soon learnt he was called for short. We'd seen some pretty impressive looking offices on our journey to this point, but Dr C's suites made all the others look like playrooms. Sitting in his busy waiting room was like sitting in the wings of a medical stage play. Staff didn't just walk in this office, they swept. And no-one swept better than Dr C himself. Before we met him personally, we watched him cross the room, back and forth, back and forth again. He swept in a flock—an immaculately dressed, efficient flock—several staff trailing behind him, but he always at the helm. And he swept so swiftly that you could almost feel the breeze brush your skin as you waited.

Unfortunately, Mike and I didn't get off to a good start with Dr C. We weren't efficient or streamlined. We didn't sweep our way in; we came in feet shuffling, heads hanging. We had broken the cardinal rule of seeing a specialist for the first time: we'd forgotten our referral. We muttered our embarrassed apologies as he sat studying us, neat and compact, emanating barely suppressed energy from behind his giant desk. We thought for a moment we might be evicted.

But then we started to tell him our story. The story of our all-stops journey, of Dr A's initial discovery, of Dr B's search and destroy mission, of my glued-together insides, and of the endometriosis that stood like a road black in our journey, like a mutating monster rearing to regrow. We expected Dr C might dismiss us at any point, fed up with our inability to follow simple procedures. But as we spoke, he leaned forward. And further forward. Before we'd reached the end of our tale, he'd ordered copies of our gory-glue photos to be sent from Dr B. A quick perusal of our scans was all that was needed before his eyes lit up. 'Your endo is severe,' he said. 'Rare, even.'

I have since learnt it is almost never a good sign when a doctor calls your condition rare.

There were areas of my insides that Dr B hadn't dared venture upon, due to their very tricky geography. Dr C had no such qualms. 'I can go there,' said Dr C. 'In fact, until we go there, we cannot be sure we have got it all, and while it is still there, it will grow again.'

We were heading to Melbourne. Dr C was based in Sydney. Suddenly we had a decision to make. Would we be willing to return for surgery just several months after our move?

Only days before we left for Melbourne, we met once more in Dr C's office. Doctors, I have learnt, are prone to eccentricity. Perhaps it's just how they cope with the life-and-death demands of their profession. Dr C was no exception. It was on this second occasion of our meeting he gave the speech I will never forget. It had all the drama and scope of a Shakespearean monologue.

'Imagine I am a pilot,' he said, 'and we are flying, and then suddenly, there is a storm! There is thunder and lightning, and I say to you, "Will you jump with me? Will you jump out of the plane?" What will you do?'

He held out his sure surgeon's hands, and I couldn't help thinking of where those hands had been, what they had done. *Will you trust me?* his expert hands implored.

I giggled nervously, an unnatural high sound, and looked sideways at Mike. What Dr C could never have known was how uncannily placed his choice of words were. Planes, medical procedures, adrenal sports. Dr C had somehow managed to fuse some of my most fearsome foes together into a sort of diabolical doctor's brew. But his promise was big: this time the endo enemy would be defeated, he seemed to be saying. Of course, there was no doubt that I wanted that. But at what expense? At what risk? He certainly had the confidence. I wouldn't want to be his opponent. But we had been hardened by painful experience. No matter what anyone told us, or how emphatically they did so, there were no guarantees.

But there was still the hope, dangled out, the prospect of possibility. Not just of a dramatic reduction to my endometriosis, but of the best preparation, at last, for my body to have a baby. And there was something else, too. There was the possibility this wasn't only in the hands of Dr C, after all.

What if this was it? What if this was the answer we'd asked for, on our knees on the carpet on New Year's Eve, as we looked out over the lake to the mountains? It was worth a try at least, wasn't it, to find out?

I took a deep breath and nodded at Mike. He nodded back. We may have held hands—we definitely held hearts—as together we decided to take the risk. We decided to get on board Dr C's crazy plane in the middle of a storm. We decided to jump. I wanted to do it; I really did. I wanted to try. But it didn't stop the fact that even just thinking about it, even just looking at the surgeon's smug, smiling face, and thinking of him flying the plane, of making the tandem jump, made the skin on my palms sweat, made the pulse in my throat flutter and speed up. Even the thought of being a passenger once more filled me with unease.

***

In late March we drove the eleven hours from Melbourne back up to Sydney in our little hatchback for my scheduled surgery.

 I lay in a white hospital bed once more, awaiting my spot on the surgical list. Perhaps due to the degree of difficulty he liked to tackle, and the bold, no-spot-off-limits approach he took to his bodily excavation work, Dr C's surgery hours were long, and we were waiting well into the afternoon. Mike sat beside my bed and talked to me as I ran my fingers nervously up and down his arm, and we watched old episodes of 'Friends' to try and pass the hours. By the time the anaesthetist came in to see me, I was about 180 degrees further in the direction of strung-out than in the morning when we arrived.

 'How are you feeling?' he asked, leaning relaxedly down over my bed. He had a friendly smile, a lean, athletic looking face. He looked like the type of doctor who rode a bike or at least went to the gym on his day off.

 'Nervous,' I replied. 'Really nervous.'

 The lack of water for so many hours, it seemed, had drained the liquid of inhibitions from me. And any ounce of courage.

 He smiled. 'You'll be fine,' he said, squeezing my arm. And then, as he left to head to the door, he turned. 'Let's do it!' he said sportingly.

 If Dr C was the overly confident captain of our journey, my anaesthetist was the cheery co-pilot, in charge of take-off and touch down. But I found his words anchoring rather than destabilising. It's amazing the effect of touch on an anxious body. That singular squeeze of my arm, the tip of a smile as he spoke his parting words, gave me hope. If I was going to go up in the air with these men, at least I knew they didn't plan on letting me go.

While my husband roamed the hospital corridors like a nervous, over-caffeinated animal, while our friends and family prayed, Dr C went intrepidly exploring, excavating endometriosis from the far reaches of my body. It turned out he really was an expert. Four long hours later, and he was finished. He left barely a remnant behind.

In the aftermath, I spent several vulnerable days in my hospital bed trying to adjust to my puffy, inflated stomach, taking my time once more to re-begin basic tasks, like walking slow laps around the hospital corridors as much as the pain would allow. Mike fondly called my hunched over shuffle in hospital gown and slippers the 'surgical strut' and walked in time beside me as staff caught our eyes and smiled kindly.

Hospital stays, no matter how short or long, remind you of the value and privilege of fresh air. Of the gift of normality. As soon as I was discharged from the hospital. we drove to the nearest beach and stood at the edge of the water. I breathed in the thick-with-salt-and-life breeze, grateful to be over the worst of it. Grateful to be heading forward into a new, more hopeful phase of our lives, or so I thought.

We attended Dr C's suites once more a few days later for a post-op appointment. He cleared me to drive home to Melbourne, so long as we took regular stops to stretch along the way.

'And now?' we asked Dr C, the unanswerable question still hanging in the air between us.

'Now we wait and see what happens next,' he said.

We'd already done a lot of waiting. Perhaps this should have set off some sort of cautionary signal to us. But it didn't. This felt different.

We had jumped from the plane with Dr C, and we had survived. More than survived. We had triumphed.

Surely this was the high point we had been waiting for. Progress had been made.

We returned to Melbourne with hope sitting between us in the car, anticipation getting out alongside us at every stop. We were returning differently to how we had left.

We were ready, we believed, for what came next.

Chapter Fifteen
Always Winter

Let's just suppose for a moment that we were able to sit down with and interview anxiety, to ask it, for instance, where it prefers to hang out in the everyday. I don't know if it would choose the beach or the snow, the country or the city. I'm not sure it actually has a favourite terrain, though I personally believe it thrives most powerfully in a lack of light, like a sturdy houseplant, and that an ample supply of Vitamin D tends to go a long way in drying it out. I remember for a long time thinking anxiety could never strike the extroverted, bubbly, sporty beings of the world, believing that the negative vibes must just bounce right off them, like Teflon, only to find my theory disproved on numerous occasions over the years. While anxiety isn't overly picky about location or individual, I do know that there are certain conditions it can, and does, latch onto more readily. As the Wise Woman explained to me once while drawing a diagram, as she often did as she spoke, while some pressure is inevitable in life, and can even be good, too much pressure, coming from too many directions at once, can trigger anxiety to wake up again. To spike to a peak. To start acting out.

Pressures like an interstate move and an invasive surgery within only months of each other; pressures like an interminable period riding the waves of uncertainty and unmet expectations; pressures like a continual, almost obsessive focus on one's body, and what it was and wasn't doing at each and every point in the month; pressures like those that came from a years-long infertility journey and life in a new city far from existing support networks.

Pressures that, for whatever reason, seemed to suddenly appear and get so much more intense, so much heavier, as the seasons changed.

***

Winter intercepted autumn and came early to Melbourne in the form of a stubborn chill, the likes of which our bodies had never before experienced. As we pulled back into St Kilda, the trees on our new street were already losing their leaves. Where they had once been thick with foliage, they were now stick-like, skeletal, stripped of their outer layers of comfort. I couldn't help but see a little of myself, of my newly excavated, still tender body, in the stark, raw stretch of their branches, in their silent, naked wait for new growth.

Our apartment, which had been such a welcome reprieve from the sear of summer, overnight became a cold shell. Worse than the lack of appropriate heating, we soon discovered that the low-lying windows let in very little natural light. With the days now turning dark early in the evening, we all spent more time at home, including the two burly men who shared the apartment above us and almost daily left us surprise gifts of cigarette butts on our doormat or held loud, techno-thumping parties far into the night. We came quickly to understand why it was we collected and accumulated so much mail addressed to so many past inhabitants of the apartment. It seemed no-one lived here for very long. Our building wasn't so much a refuge as a place no-one wanted to stay and put down roots.

And so too, it seemed, was my body. Despite the surgery, which Dr C had declared a triumphant success, despite our initial renewed hopeful anticipation, month after month passed, and we began to feel like little more than unwilling sponsors of the pregnancy test industry. Always buying, never getting any pay-off. No matter what brand we bought, the ones with the cross or the ones with the line, no matter how I administered them, the dippy stick in the little plastic cup or over the toilet, the end result was the same every time. Blank. And as I threw the used kits in the bin, I felt my hope, bit by bit, being buried in there along with them.

***

The pressures upon us that year were big and longstanding, and they were unexpected and random. One day at the city church we had started attending, we were introduced to a young family visiting. In an effort to be welcoming and warm, knowing what it felt like to be the newcomers, we reached out our hands to shake theirs. The following night, at almost exactly the same moment, both Mike and I started feeling nauseous. Together we raced for our single bathroom. I only made it as far as the sink. We shivered our way feverishly through that night, side by side. Though Mike recovered quickly and returned to work, my body didn't bounce back quite so easily. I lay alone at home on the couch in our dimly lit bunker of an apartment, the window lifted just a little to let a sliver of fresh air in, but not too much to blow me away.

In the unfortunate collision of post-surgery recovery and stomach flu, my long, stubbornly held association between sickness and anxiety resurfaced with unexpected force. Illness susceptibility, something I had struggled with on and off since childhood, the product of a vivid imagination powerfully re-ignited by the seemingly endless 'what if' impulses of anxiety, came in swinging.

One afternoon when stomach cramps were particularly strong, and Mike wasn't answering his phone, I frantically googled symptoms, terrified I had contracted a post-surgical infection or, worse, that I was dying. Something the Wise Woman had told me echoed in the back of my mind, but the message was faint. *It is always best to first picture the most likely scenario*, she said, *not the worst.* The most probable reason for the stomach cramps was that I was just unwell, still suffering from the effects of a strong bug. I wasn't dying, I was just sick. But I couldn't calm down long enough to heed her words with any clarity, to see the distinctions.

If hypochondria was my erratic heartbeat in that season, shame was my constant shadow. As a veteran anxiety sufferer, I thought I should have been able to do better, even with all the challenges coming our way. I knew about the dangers of avoidance, of the need for accepting my feelings if I wanted to survive them. I'd not only learnt it all before; I'd practised it too. I'd sat with the pain of my own intense adrenaline on the aeroplane to New York and I'd called anxiety out. I'd faced down my fears time and time again, and risen from my bed, from the bath, from my knees. But that winter buffeted all the bluff from me.

Like the cold wind tunnel that signalled the entrance to Mike's new workplace, I felt like my body was hollow and chaotic, a victim of every breeze that blew. With no workplace of my own in this new city, I followed Mike around like a mewling stray cat, carting my books and my heavy laptop with me like rocks on my back, while my stomach played up in a dance with my adrenaline that seemed never to settle. At my worst I sat outside Mike's classrooms, just to be near to him, trying to blend in with the carefree students around me, casually pretending to work on my dissertation research and writing while a giant bundle of overactive adrenal glands pulsed inside me.

A couple of years earlier, my mother had suffered her own acute attack of PD, her personal and particular journey with grizzle-faced GAD. It was after her heart attack, after her autoimmune disease diagnosis. She was in hospital once more, worried about a new pain in her chest, a pain it turned out, this time, was most likely caused by anxiety and the still-abrasive rub of grief rather than any other new physical problems. But with her colourful history, the medical staff didn't want to take any chances. I remember visiting her in her hospital room, Mike close beside me, and seeing it on her face, the shadow of swarming darkness, the look of one who had gone down into the pit, despite being elevated by a pile of white pillows. It was a story I could read easily because it reflected so precisely parts of my own. I knew where she was, and I longed to break her from it. I wanted to reach my arm down and literally pull her out. It felt impossibly heavy, to see my own enemy on the face of my mother, invading her too.

That look on my mother's face, of blank fear, of despair, of her descent into darkness: when I look at photos of our year in Melbourne, the year between our second round of surgery and nearly giving up, that's what I see in me too. I see it in the way I stand, my shoulders raised too high, my smile too forced, trying to cover up the layer of pain just beneath, trying to hold up the roof of my world from caving in.

And I remember, too, how it felt. How I wanted nothing more than for someone to take the weight from me.

To reach down deep to where I had fallen and pull me back up.

***

At times, as I shared some of my struggles, people offered to pray for me, or pointed me to what they believed would be strong, fortifying verses, sturdy, standalone nuggets of comfort hewn for hard times. They were the sort of phrases that I'd written for years in diaries and notebooks or stuck on my wall with blue tack, classics like Philippians 4:6, easily called to mind by the childhood phrase 'when in a fix, turn to Philippians 4:6'. Or Romans 8, where all things worked together for good. At best, I felt the love in the attempts to help me; at worst, I felt like I was not only physically unwell, but spiritually too, stranded helpless on a stretcher in some sort of Christianese speaking hospital. Everyone wanted to fix me, with an injection of quick hope, a dose of wise counsel, a few well-timed intercessions—only, none of the cures seemed to be working. The problem wasn't that I didn't know or remember what my Bible said in these extracted pieces, but that I wasn't sure anymore how to think about them, especially when it came to seeing how exactly they applied to me. Where was the peace that passed understanding when I was stranded breathless in the bathroom? It definitely didn't feel like that in me. It was all well and good to say that all worked together for good, but what if I no longer had the strength to see this? What happened, too, with all the bad?

On top of the highly ill-timed return of my old anxiety symptoms, I had a new problem, one I had no official diagnosis for but felt strongly. Perhaps it could be called acute spiritual anxiety. Even reading the Bible, at this point in time, felt like too much. Every time I picked up my reliable NIV, ESV or any other translation that I had carried from Sydney to Melbourne and that I now kept facing out on our bookshelves (I had them all, and also all the study guides), I felt bombarded by my own inadequacy. I harboured a heavy lump of guilt and remorse at my seeming inability to summon any faith or hope to get me through to the other side of my slump of fear and darkness. Like any Christian perfectionist, I knew my chapter and verses on suffering. But rather than words of comfort, of encouragement, to my ears they started to sound like a string of commands that I was failing at. Why couldn't I just trust, and obey, and be okay? If I believed in an all-powerful, all-loving God, then why couldn't I even work in the library on my own without feeling like the walls were closing in on me? If every fibre of me was on fire with fear, was there even any room left inside of me for faith? Did I still trust God? Even scarier: did God still love me?

The truth was, anxiety didn't sit outside my relationship with God, as I suppose I expected or wanted it to. It came in there too. Anxiety, especially during that season of pressure, made me second guess everything, until even my own faith felt uneasy, like the disciples in the boat during the storm, only I didn't know if Jesus was awake for me. Or if I knew it, I struggled to feel it in all the rocking. Was God the father in the prodigal story, with his arms outstretched waiting to welcome me home again from the long distance I'd travelled, or a disappointed parent, wagging his finger at me while I hung my head in shame? If I knew he was the first, I often felt he was the second.

And meanwhile, the external, earthly hits just kept coming.

***

Late one night we received a call from my mum. Her voice was urgent, off kilter. Dad had gone in for a routine check-up with his cardiologist and had not been allowed to leave the hospital. He needed urgent surgery. The news shocked and confronted me. It seemed not that long ago we'd been in hospital for Mum. And now the second of my parents' hearts was breaking. We left for Sydney immediately, driving through the night, hoping to make it to be with Mum before Dad went under. Our little blue car faithfully covered the kilometres between our new home and our old home yet again, once more on a form of medical mission. I dozed fitfully as Mike kept his eyes on the road. We stopped for food and drinks at odd hours, thankful for twenty-four-hour refuges like McDonalds, no matter what anyone thought of their nutritional validity. But I couldn't eat much more than a small burger and a lemonade. In the stark, over-exposing light of a truck-stop bathroom, I examined the protruding line of my ribs through my T-shirt. I was losing weight again. And I wasn't even trying.

We held our breaths and prayed, and Dad's quadruple bypass went well. We were able to visit him several days later. He was his usual, stoic self, even when covered in cords and attached to machines that beamed his stats to screens and beeped disconcertingly for those of us who didn't speak their erratic language. He was tired, of course, and the strong drugs he was on to recover caused him to see things out of order. One time he asked the nurse to get his wife. 'She's not here right now,' the nurse replied.

'Yes, she is,' he corrected her. 'She's over there.' He patiently pointed to a bunch of flowers bobbing in as vase on the bedside table.

'I can't believe I actually thought your mother was a flower,' he laughed incredulously with us after.

It was a strange, surreal, tender time.

Gradually Dad improved and was able to leave hospital. He began a daily regimen of walking. First, just a few metres down the road, then a little more, and more. When learning to live again, even a few steps is a big deal.

But while my father was walking slowly forwards, I felt like I was going backwards.

We returned once more on the long road to Melbourne. To the stubbornly persistent winter. To an increasingly busy workload for Mike that demanded his full attention. Away from the immediate focus on my father, my anxiety lumbered back in like a squatter. And I began to question if my most recent surgery had even been worth it. If Dr C was such a reputed miracle worker, why hadn't his plane-in-the-storm stunt worked for me?

As anxiety took up more and more space inside me, my world didn't just shrink, it took on a new shape altogether. Nowhere felt safe anymore. Not the university, not our cold apartment. Even church, always a place of centring and comfort, now felt strange. I couldn't raise my hands, let alone my head, to sing. And one particularly hard night, I had my first panic attack ever inside a church building and could barely get myself to leave the bathroom. I emerged, shaking, to the buzzing post-service crowd, my eyes streaming tears. Even in God's house, surrounded by his people, I no longer felt safe. But if I couldn't go there for security, I asked myself, then where was there left to go?

***

I tried all I could think of to feel better. To get better. To climb out of the hollow ground with my two trembling arms.

I tried a new psychologist a few suburbs away that required I walk for 40 minutes just to get there. I could have taken a tram, of course, but that would have called for the mental energy to figure out the stops and the system, and I didn't have even that in reserve. The counsellor's office itself was a large room in a gloomy brown-brick building that would have made a great setting for a gothic movie. Two chairs seemed to float suspended on a small carpet in the middle of the room, and a miniature heater wheezed noisily to puff out warm air. I chewed peppermints from the front desk as I spoke and listened and attempted to take the tiniest bit of information in. But even talking didn't seem to help anymore. The words passed through me as I sat there and were swallowed into the night sky as I left.

I tried yoga, in a trendy upstairs studio above an organic cafe, with a male instructor who wore full-length purple lycra tights (which would have been hilarious if I could still laugh) and welcomed us ceremoniously, promising relief. Somehow, everyone else seemed to know exactly what they were doing: when to bend, how far to extend, where to leave their shoes when they entered. I stood at the back of the room struggling to keep up, limbs weak only ten minutes in, drawing the concerned attention of the purple-legged man. What was meant to make me feel calmer only made me feel more unstable.

I tried physiotherapy and osteopathy. I tried an expensive gym membership that amounted to nothing more than money disappearing from our bank account each month. I tried mantras and herbs. We bought a new orthopaedic mattress that was 'guaranteed' to help us rest easy.

I tried medicine, when an eccentric local GP, who was more used to working with local drug addicts than anxious wannabe mothers, prescribed me diazepam to be taken on the spot 'as needed'. I remember picking the little white bottle of tablets up from the chemist one night and feeling instant relief. But once ingested into my thin frame, the medicine ran riot. One day I sat in a park in a patch of sun, the sounds of happy families all around me, and worked on reading for my dissertation—only to find the next day when I looked over my notes that I couldn't remember even writing them.

'I'm not sure if the medicine is working too well,' Mike suggested diplomatically a few days in, noting my constantly spaced-out state, my slow gait as I walked behind him, my increased irritability and irrationality in conversation. 'I think he must have given you too high a dose. Did he even weigh you?'

At first, I resisted my husband's words. At least when I was on the tablets, I didn't feel the pain as intensely, I could sleep through the night. And often through the day, too. But he was right, they weren't helping me to live so much as drawing life from me, making me feel constantly hungover. So I stopped taking them.

There was a lake I visited at that time in the centre of Mike's campus. I was drawn to it each day when my emotions felt too much to be contained in the walls of the ugly library building, or the wind tunnel of a cafeteria. I walked often around that lake with tears streaming, drawing in ragged breaths, trying my hardest to make the oxygen flow longer and fuller within me to all the places that questioned and ached. I tried to focus on the small band of ducks that walked around the lake together, a mother and her children, I imagined. But even they couldn't bring me back down to the solidness of the earth. I had forgotten how much anxiety could feel like pain, pressing down on me. My back ached. My gut ached. My neck ached. Even the circle of my wrist felt tense and sore.

As I made my way around the lake in repetitive, helpless circles, there was one thing that soothed me, at least a little. Listening to music. I remembered how much strength and support my brother had always drawn from the lyrics of songs, from the unaccountable comfort of melody when nothing else could penetrate. How sometimes in the car, as he drove me places, the two of us would share our own 'concerts', playing songs to one another we felt said things that were sometimes unsayable. One of the last things he wrote out in a letter to me were the lyrics of the song 'Sister' by The Nixons, about the shared love that exists, regardless of time, or distance. Or death. There is a certain power in music, I'm sure, that is on another plane than the rational or explainable, that is God-given.

I played a variety of songs and artists on those long, loopy lakeside walks, ones Greg and I had shared, classics like Randy Stonehill's 'Hymn', which we had played on the first anniversary of the accident. But I was drawn most of all to one song in particular, and I sent it over and over again through my earbuds. It was one my mother-in-law, Roz, had helpfully pointed me to: 'Spring is coming' by Steven Curtis Chapman. It reminded me of something Greg once penned in a letter to me, that 'nothing lasts forever, both the good and the bad'. And that eventually the seasons shift.

Even the longest and toughest of seasons.

Like C. S. Lewis's famous frozen Narnian landscape, that year in Melbourne we, too, seemed to be caught in an always winter, never Christmas reality-unreality, and if Aslan was on the move, I struggled most of the time to see signs of him. But sometimes I sensed him, behind the scenes, in the music, in the groaning prayers of the Spirit on my behalf when I no longer had the energy for words. At last, when none of my own efforts were enough to make the season shift, to release me from the state of deep freeze I found myself in, I did the last thing left. I waited. And I squintingly watched.

For spring.

For hope.

For Aslan himself to appear and melt the snow.

Chapter Sixteen

Friends Like Penguins

E ven now, fragments of my brother's words return to me unbidden at odd times, or in significant moments, comforting me, reorienting me, guiding me forward. Like remnants of a home I've left behind, they point me onward to a place I am yet to reach. I wonder if it will always be this way. I suspect it will. No matter how far I travel from our beginning, my brother's words journey inside me. An anchor, a key, a compass.

Greg once told me that he believed that sometimes, when we cannot see God or feel his presence, he sends people in his place to be his hands, his arms, his steady heartbeat. His message of hope packaged in imperfect, unique, earthly vessels. When we aren't sure anymore if he's even with us, he appears at our shoulder in the tangible ordinary mystery of the prayers, tears, and laughter of our relationships.

After we finished school, unwilling for the richness of our years spent in youth group together to end, my girlfriends and I formed a prayer group. For close to a decade, we met fortnightly at one another's houses. Together, in that group, we discovered what it is to bear one another's burdens, to cry over tea and cake, to laugh until our sides split and we felt understood.

In our individual particularity. In our communal finiteness. We talked, we shared, we prayed. We journeyed through young adulthood and dating, for some of us marriage, and kids; and now, so many years later, we stand on the threshold of middle age, scattered across the globe, technology enabling us to keep in touch and have each other's backs.

About a year before we left Sydney, Emma gave me a card. She told just how much sorrow she was feeling alongside me in our fertility struggles. She said she had even dreamt about me the last few nights. And that the words of Psalm 113 had come to her, and that she'd told them to me. This wasn't trite Bible flipping. I felt her words and the psalm as almost prophetic. The front of the card itself was beautiful. A picture of a slim girl/woman in a duffle coat and long skirt, with wavy brown, tousled hair bracing against the wind, on a muted gold background. There was something uncannily familiar about her. But it was the details of the image that stood out most of all. Above her head, following her, a small troop of paper planes, as if they were pushing her on, escorting her, helping her walk. The artist, it said on the back, was from Melbourne. The paper planes, I imagined, were like my friends' prayers, behind me in that time, helping me to keep moving through the wind.

That cold year in Melbourne, I remember walking the long, draughty corridors of Mike's university campus, my old-fashioned brick of a phone in hand (a teenage shop assistant once asked if I was holding a walkie-talkie), calling one after another of my prayer group friends in Sydney, often in the very midst of panic attacks. They were always supportive, talking me through like they had done so many times before. Their voices became my stepping stones at that time, their patient, listening ears my bridge spanning turbulent waters. And as a couple, Mike and I made new friends too, in the new city, wonderful partnerships like Simon and Susan and James and Tracey who fed us, encouraged us, and made us laugh. Our friendships were young and tender, and I had very little inside me to invest, but we dwelt together as best we could. And what were once small seeds have now, years later, in another time and place, budded growth in directions we never expected.

But there was one unlikely friendship in that dark Melbourne year that seemed, for want of any other word, to be providential. In the midst of our gritty urban valley, God reached into his pocket and selected for us one of his most interesting and beloved children to walk beside us.

***

God sent Pilgrim to us one evening at church. In itself this does not sound so unusual, but Pilgrim did not regularly attend our Melbourne church; she was just visiting from her residential accommodation at a university across town. She had peddled her bike through the cold, wet air, for almost an hour to be there. She *happened* to sit in the row in front of us and we *happened* to be in a friendly enough mood to introduce ourselves. The girl who turned around had short, bobbed hair, a sassy, wide smile, and a quirky, eclectic dress style. In Melbourne, we very quickly learnt, people favoured a fashion of all black. It was almost a uniform. Chic, sophisticated, monochrome as the winter sky. Pilgrim blew in in a patchwork of colour. Her origins were patchwork too. She was a Dutch PhD student, studying in Melbourne but en route from China where she planned to return and work when her doctorate was complete.

She laughed and praised our fumbling, eager attempts at Dutch, as Mike tried out his repertoire of phrases learnt from spending time in Holland on holiday with my young nieces and nephews. Sometimes, in a new environment, relationships fast track where in familiarity they might plod. We exchanged phone numbers and made on the spot plans to visit

Phillip Island together in a couple of weekends' time, a wild, scenic destination off the coast of Melbourne where tourists like us flocked to watch the colony of penguins come in from the surf at sunset.

Pilgrim arrived at our apartment a few weeks later by train, and together we drove to the island, our windows open and filled with wide sky vistas and pastoral, postcard-worthy hills. Though we had come from such different places, we found quickly that we shared unusual commonalities amongst our very contrasting lives. We talked about music, art, theology, language. Pilgrim was the first person I'd met in Melbourne, or elsewhere, who knew of the writing of Brennan Manning, of the music of Rich Mullins. She read Eugene Peterson and knew of the European theologians Mike was working on. She sat in the back of our small car, but leant forward as she spoke, and our words flowed in a stream of reciprocity.

Without wanting to turn her into a saint, Pilgrim was different from anyone else we had ever met. For a start, nothing about her everyday life was conventional: she was single and childless and unperturbed about it; while her large family still lived in Holland, she balanced her life between three countries without obvious unsteadiness. Her career path itself was based on an upside-down logic, all about taking risks for the kingdom of God in obscure, out-of-the-way places where she would not garner any credit for doing it. She had an unhurried peace, a secure sure-footedness, and just being around her somehow had an ability to calm me. She didn't own a television and rarely interacted on social media. She had friends all over the world but didn't seem to miss her home. We joked, for a while there, that perhaps she was an angel. If so, then we were so far on the right track with her. Didn't the Bible tell us to offer hospitality to such as these? Whether she had secret wings or not, she was definitely the most untethered person I'd met, and similarly the most grounded. She literally carried her backpack from place to place, from home to home. But what stood out most of all was her comfort in her own God-given skin. This would have stood out at any time, of course, but at a time when I literally squirmed in my own, it did so all the more.

We crossed over the long bridge to the island as pastel colour began to marble the sky and arrived just in time to buy tickets to see the penguins do their thing for the eager humans. After sharing a large bowl of hot chips dipped in mayonnaise, a very Dutch delicacy, we moved outside to witness the sunset parade.

So popular are the penguins in their evening crossing from sea to their land burrows that stadium seating is set up for the event. We were late coming in, so we didn't get a bench seat, but we found a spot for the three of us on the sloped ground. Mike had brought a picnic blanket, and we spread it out like a carpet on the soft grass.

At first, as we leant forward to watch, just a few little black-and-white bodies surfaced in the shallows. Like so many bowling skittles, they gathered in the foam. Others soon came to join them, buffeted into the shore from the ocean. They waited, it appeared, until they deemed enough members of their kind to have joined them. And then, like an extended family crossing a busy road, they joined numbers and waddled across the sand's surface together. We cheered as they made the crossing from water to land. Sometimes a lone penguin would surface at the edge of the sand, only to get washed back out to sea again, necessitating them to try the whole exercise once more. These we felt particular sympathy for. Even more rarely, one would make it across alone, scuttling forward rigid and hesitant, wings flailing at its side. But after watching the penguins' movements for only a short time, something became very clear: it was the company, the communion with others at this sunset hour, that gave them the most courage, that brought the majority safely to shore.

It grew increasingly cold as we sat on the ground and strained our eyes to see the movement before us. We wore beanies and scarves, but even still the wind bit at the chinks in our woollen armour, and my back ached from my recent surgery and stress. But in that moment, I felt something I hadn't felt for months. My panic receded, swallowed into the shallows, and I was able to drink it all in for a while… a wash of light. In Dutch, there is a word we do not have an accurate translation for in English. It denotes contentedness, not necessarily based on circumstance, or even surroundings, but on the warmth that comes from togetherness: *gezellig*. It means convivial, cosy, intimate, snug, warm. That moment, with my husband by my shoulder on one side and my new friend on the other, felt all these things and more.

Eventually, when no more penguin bodies emerged valiant from the ocean, we stood. We wove our slow way up the hill as all around us the little black-and-white community continued to find their way to their burrows. Waving our little torchlights in the darkening night, we wished them well, audibly sighing as we saw them find their earthy nests. It is a good and beautiful thing to watch a creature find its place in the world, no matter how transitory. It is even better to see them do it with the help of their friends.

We drove back home again along that long, winding, picturesque road, the car once more pleasantly full but now with quieter, slower conversation. Dropping Pilgrim at the train station where she'd parked her bike, we watched as she unlocked her chain, switched on her headlight, and headed home. A small, moving pool of light in a dark night.

After that first visit, Pilgrim became a solid friend. Some of our favourite moments were visiting places together, like the Dandenong Ranges, with their enchanting mountain towns, their tall trees and forest; it became one of our favourite spots. On one such trip, we had a conversation I'll never forget.

'My nerves are jangled,' I said aloud into the car, not sure if I was speaking to Mike, or Pilgrim, or just needing to voice it for myself.

Pilgrim wasted no time replying from the back, 'Then just let them dangle.'

Let them dangle. The words immediately struck me.

Mike later pointed out that Pilgrim's words, whether intended or not, were uncannily close to those of one of my favourite verses. 'Be still, and know that I am God!' (Ps 46:10) could be translated, Mike explained, to 'let it dangle, and know that I am God'.

Don't try and fix everything all the time, don't try to straitjacket your nerves and tie them so tight that they strain at the edges, don't even wish to wish them away. Just accept how you feel and know that one greater holds you. Pilgrim didn't say this second part, but I knew that was the strength of the meaning bolstering her words. It is such a great image, and it has stuck with me since. Later that afternoon, as we wandered a small coastal village, my nerves swaying gently in the breeze, unfettered and remarkably—as it turned out—unfazed, Pilgrim took out her camera and took photos of what we affectionately termed 'dangles'. Symbols of our effort to let the loose threads of life hang, like brambly branches, from the vine of our Father.

Before spring arrived later that year, Pilgrim travelled back to China. I missed her, but I also felt so much richer for our time together.

Pilgrim is just one of those fellow penguins, those torch-bearing co-travellers, who have helped me cross from the waves to the shore over the years. And in that year, in those few key months, she played a role in stopping me, I'm convinced, from being washed back into the water altogether, from going back under.

PART IV: THE DEEP

The water there is of a blue
more brilliant than sapphire
and like I said   my lake is deep

For it would take all the aching beauty of a
deep   blue   lake
to say it all

—GVDK

Chapter Seventeen

By Christmas

Perhaps for obvious reasons, Christians love to share answers to prayer with one another. To point and say, 'Look, there! There is where I asked for God's help, and he replied.' We recount them triumphantly, as if it's the way things should be between us and God, this perfect recipe for supplication and supply. We like to draw lines too, neatly, between A and B, perhaps even with tick boxes prefigured that we can scratch off, like a spiritual accounting system. And sometimes the answer really is very obvious, very clear, very black and white. But more often than not, at least I have found, the lines that travel between request and response are wrigglier, more like a three-year-old's scribble than a mathematician's equation. Sometimes, the answer is not an answer but a denial, a 'no' to the hopes we hold, to the dreams we carry. And other times, answers come not immediately but at the end of much waiting, and in entirely unpredictable ways. Ways that defy the box, that are almost beyond tracing. Sometimes, even, they come in the form of curly-haired strangers met almost by chance at the end of long roads, strangers who could have no way of knowing that they hold the signposts, that they are the unexpected reply.

***

When my body took much longer than I hoped to recover, I sought out a new GP in the neighbouring, more affluent, suburb of Elwood. If St Kilda was transient and trendy, the preferred locale of backpackers and bohemians and, yes, drug addicts, Elwood was the suburbs. Solid, secure, and family friendly. In tiny ways it reminded me of where I'd grown up in Sydney, and without realising it perhaps this is what drew me to it. A nostalgia for a rootedness, a safety, I felt I had lost.

A distinct feature of the area we lived in then was that it had a small canal system running through it. These and other echoes of Europe appealed to me when we first moved in, like the pastry shop on the main road run by the same family for decades, windows always packed with exotic culinary enticements, or the hubbub and flow of the trams at all hours. So many more people relied on bicycles over cars here, and along with the distinct smell of wood smoke in the air by the pier and the number of cafes that sold pancakes at all times of the day, I could almost close my eyes and see Holland. But right then, I wanted home.

I followed the path of a canal nearby our apartment to the doctor's door. It was a slow, meditative walk, due not just to my feeling of sickness, but to the heaviness I felt all over. Perhaps it was the weight of nervous hope I carried in my pockets, with their double stitch of disillusionment. I had seen so many medical professionals of late. Could I expect this one to help me any more than any of the others? Was my problem even physical anyway, or had my mind so taken over my body that the web was too hard to unpick? With these questions, I opened the door to the small suburban waiting room and closed it again on the cold day.

I couldn't have planned it, even if I had tried. The GP who came out to greet me and steer me into her office also happened to be a writer and, beyond that, a sympathetic soul. Unalarmed and unsurprised, she listened to more than my surface, current problems, and read the tensions of the plot line beneath as I sought to deliver it. Six months after the wonder-surgery with Dr C, and with still no movements on the fertility front, it was she who came up with a suggestion for our next action step. To be honest, without her, I'm not sure if we would have moved at all. As I said, answers to prayer come in all shapes and sizes. And from all directions. In this case it was a zany GP with a particularly keen intuition and fondness for fellow oddballs.

'What did the surgeon recommend you do next?' she asked, not content with the vagueness of my description of our last appointment with him.

I gave her my honest answer. 'I don't know.' Despite the fact that he had seen my deepest inside spaces, I was still a little in awe of Dr C. He'd told us to wait; it hadn't crossed my mind to press, to ask, for anything more.

'Let's ring him and find out,' she said decisively.

I watched as she found his number on her computer screen and without hesitation picked up the phone to dial the number of his suites. I could just picture his face as she demanded she speak with him, relaying what I had told her about my continued feelings of sickness about our lack of baby-making success.

After only a couple of moments (Dr C, I knew, talked fast) she put down the receiver. 'It's been over six months since your surgery,' she said. 'So he suggests making the next move.'

She looked at me pointedly.

'You mean IVF?' I filled in when it didn't seem like she would.

'It's now or never,' she replied. Actually, that's not exactly true. She didn't really say it like that. She was a writer in her downtime, but she still spoke like a doctor in the office. But that was the basic gist of it. We'd been waiting long enough. We knew it, she knew it. And she wasn't afraid to say it out loud.

One of the problems with taking so long to deliberately make a baby is that you have so much time to think, to ruminate, to stew. Of course, we'd thought about IVF, we'd talked it over with friends, we'd read up, as much as we could handle, on the ethics of it all. On the pros and cons and puddles of foggy grey matter in between. But we hadn't yet committed to the process.

'Maybe we should wait just a tiny a bit more,' I suggested. 'At least until I'm better?'

My new GP looked at me, point blank. She was kind and empathetic, but she didn't pull any punches. Not with her words. Or her eyes.

'What if the waiting is part of what's making you unwell?' she said. 'Anxiety thrives when living in limbo. Why not give it something more decisive to work with? If not now, when? You've waited long enough, right? You want to know if it's going to work, right? Well, why not find out?'

I stared back at her, hesitant and blinking.

'I have a good friend from my university days,' she told me, her voice softening into a smile. 'I think he may be able to help you.' She picked up the phone once more, and while I sat there, focusing nervously on my hands, shifting uncomfortably in my seat, wondering how many problems she'd helped solve today and if she ever got tired of hearing so much of the world's mess and trying to tidy it up, she made the call that changed our lives.

In under two minutes, the first minute mostly filled with laughter and small talk, my new GP had landed us a meeting with Dr D, one of Melbourne's top fertility experts. I only found out much later, from a nurse in the know, that his waiting list is normally at least half a year long. We had a meeting with him scheduled for just two weeks after the GP's spontaneous phone call.

***

Dr D had a disarmingly friendly face despite his senior position and, in stark contrast to Dr C's elaborate medical emporium, a simple, understated office. He was one of those rare, perplexing people who made everything, even the most difficult and delicate of matters, seem easy. In this way, his continual cool calm burst a few of our early tension bubbles. He looked at my results and listened to our story as we told it, yet again. Anyone with a chronic condition knows the pain, the weight, the exhaustion, of endless repetition. Thankfully, Dr D only needed the summary version to understand. He noted Dr C's excellent groundwork. And when we asked him for his honest opinion, he gave us his honest, unadorned answer.

'Without extra help,' he said, 'you have less than half a percentage of a chance to have a child.' We laughed at the outrageousness of the statistic, a dust mite of a probability flying through space. He simply smiled back at us, quietly, steadily. If we decided to go through with it, he said, he'd try to help us. He'd try to help us become pregnant by Christmas.

There was something about the endpoint of his timeline that stood out to me, so quaint, so hopeful. So much like a miracle. But after everything that had happened, did I even possess the energy anymore to believe?

***

Deciding whether or not to do IVF is a huge decision, worthy of another book. There are other people I believe who could tell that particular story better, and everyone's story would itself be unique. Perhaps part of the unease around fertility treatment is that there is no perfect decision.

In the end we did the best we could with what we knew and what we had been offered. We moved forward with quiet hope. And a renewed intensity of prayer.

Surprisingly, or perhaps not, my GP was right. IVF was for me, in the context I found myself in, at least no worse emotionally from what I had already been coping with. There was a rhythm, a meticulous order to it that gave me a strange comfort. We were told exactly what to do, when to turn up, and measured and watched in a way that perhaps in another scenario would have raised my anxiety, but in this case made me feel accounted for, on the way to somewhere—even if that somewhere was still unknown. As my GP said, we were, at last, doing something, and the doing something gave us momentum.

The strange world of fertility treatment was in many ways like a conveyer belt. There were entrances and exits to be followed, and each couple or individual was on a different stage of the same journey. Sometimes in the waiting room, as we all sat in our separate chairs, mentally preparing for our separate steps, I felt like we were all connected somehow. A large, conflicted web of disillusionment and anticipation. I've no doubt everyone has their own story, but for our part every one of the staff we met were caring and calm and made us feel comfortable. There was an order, a balance to it all. We prayed and we felt moved to move, and mostly, perhaps due to the rigour of it all, I managed to stay in the moment.

And even though it was only ever us at the appointments, we weren't alone. We'd been in touch with the Wise Woman about our latest decision, and she wrote us the kindest letter in return, offering something beyond even her psychological support: her personal prayers for our new leg of the journey. We wrote our family and friends regular updates on our progress, and they helped, too, to pray us through with stepping-stone prayers, often when we ourselves couldn't do much more than stretch out our arms while we tried to keep our balance.

***

When the phone call came in the midsummer month of early December, I was lying on one of the small couches in our living room, closest to the fan, wanting to feel the air on my face. I mouthed the words to Mike across the room from me as the nurse spoke, and I watched his jaw drop, as my own did too, I'm sure, while I struggled to take the information in.

After several long months of hormone injections into the soft skin of my stomach while we watched episodes of *Seinfeld* to offset the moment the needle pierced my flesh; after almost daily blood tests that became as routinely expected as morning tea; after a multitude of meetings with specialised nursing staff, some of whose job descriptions I never even knew existed until this moment; after mandatory fertility counselling and suggested beneficial acupuncture; after walks through the rain by the Yarra River and vegetarian burgers sitting cross legged on our bed together afterwards, because it was all I felt like eating for some reason; after reading up on the procedures and trying not to read too much into the procedures; after weighing statistics and risks and, in the end, not knowing if any of it would even ever come to anything; after the tremors of day surgery and the moment of release into anaesthetic; after prayers, and messages, and more prayers and more messages, sent out like smoke signals into the darkest of nights, when the cloud cover sometimes obscured even the pinprick light of the stars… an embryo was returned to my body, and that embryo become a tiny seed of life inside me.

I remember the celebratory meal we took after we received the nurse's phone call, at a bayside cafe perched where the land leant over the water, our startled bodies turned in to the fresh spring wind. When we finished eating, we walked hand in hand across a stretch of bright green grass, still shiny from rain, watching the birds cross the midday sky delivering messages to one another, the language of which we would never understand. We composed our own messages too, to our friends and family, and drank in the amazed responses of joy as they came back at us, adorned with kisses and promises of embraces when we were together again, like the dessert course of our meal. We weren't the only ones to cry drought-breaking tears that afternoon.

None of us, least of all Mike and I, were unaware that the messages, the responses, the delicious icing of celebration, could have all have gone very differently. There was a profound fragility in the awareness of our new situation. In many ways, joy, and its near neighbour sorrow, had never seemed closer. And for a moment, I even felt guilty. Why us and not others? During our time immersed in the world of fertility treatments, we had seen what felt like the Russian roulette system of it all. Some people came out of the cycle, like us now, rising to celebration, while others were sent back down to the ground. We were standing in the middle of a miracle, yes, but we knew it wasn't one we could ever have demanded as somehow our right. I couldn't help thinking of all the other journeys breaking down just as ours was gaining momentum. God could just as easily have closed the door. But he hadn't, and we were, in the moment, very, very thankful. He had handed us possibility, and we stretched out our arms to take it.

And then, we held it very, very close.

With this news cradled tenderly and vulnerably to our hearts, we made an important decision. With regret, Mike gave notice to his university in

Melbourne. One thing had become very clear to us. We couldn't stay where we were. Not any longer. Not now. Mike's brother Rich flew in to help us, along with a dear cousin who lived across the city, and the contents of our difficult, complex year were bundled efficiently into boxes and taped together, our team of helpers literally bearing the burden of our departure.

The night before we left, completely unexpectedly, our friends James and Tracey from our Melbourne church knocked on our door. 'We are so sorry we couldn't help more with the packing,' they said.

We reassured them it was fine. They held out an envelope. 'Something to help you in your transition,' they said.

It wasn't until they left that we opened the envelope and read the kind card. And something else popped out too. Five hundred dollars, money we needed to help with our sudden change of plans. I was acutely aware of what sort of friend I'd been to Tracey, patchy and inconsistent, sometimes there, often absent. But they offered the gift without reservation. Grace for our travels.

James and Tracey's gift made sense on another level too. It was a little like Melbourne for us. We'd run there, trying to escape, and run instead into unexpected obstacles. But in the end, it was the unexpected gifts that found us anyway. Like friendship and positive pregnancy tests. And grace that shone brighter and richer for the grit.

It was Christmas Eve when we pulled out of our street in St Kilda for the last time. The trees were once more clothed in a rich, full cover of green. With the help of another maybe-angel called Ned, we drove across the border and into the evening. Ned was a wiry, industrious sole operator and the best removalist we've ever worked with. Powered only by fruit juice and ingenuity, he had our stuff on his truck in Victoria and off again in New South Wales by lunchtime the next day.

It was the twenty-fifth of December. The sun shone down on us from a bright, clear blue sky.

Winter had finally ended.

Christmas had arrived at last.

Chapter Eighteen

Even on Mountaintops

When maybe-angel removalist Ned stepped down the ramp of his truck on Christmas morning and planted his boots firmly on the scrubby grass of our new, temporary home, he smiled. 'This is better,' he said as he surveyed the view.

Indeed, it appeared to be so.

The sky was wide and impossibly blue, and even the air had a different smell: fresher, purer, the way air should smell, I thought. Like God's breath.

I spread my arms out to let it pass over me.

After we left Melbourne with new life hidden fresh and fragile in my belly, we didn't feel quite ready yet to return to the busyness of Sydney. Though we wanted to go home, we also felt like we needed a bit of space, a place to hide out for a while and process the year that had been, and to prepare for what was to come. Our internal as well as our external compasses led us to the sublime, rugged escarpment of the New South Wales Blue Mountains, less than two hours from the city. To the Three Sisters in their ancient, solemn alignment. To the embrace of the bush and the magical blue haze of eucalypt.

We found a short-term rental cottage nestled in the trees in cosy Katoomba, or K-Town as the locals called it. This was a place where nature was big but everything else was far smaller. And we were glad for the grandness, thankful for our little temporary wooden nest. For three months, we planned to do little more than read, rest, and write. Mike needed to finish his doctorate, and I needed to make my way slowly back into mine again while giving space to the other nest, the one my body had now become. We needed time, too, to think our way forward to other off-page, still-in-progress life decisions. We knew what we left behind, but not what we travelled towards. Work, housing, church. These were all, once more, unknowns. The future was foggy, like the thick mist that regularly pooled and floated around our car as we drove along the winding mountain roads. Though it concealed our path, for a time, we didn't mind the valley haze. It felt more like a covering than an obstruction. A way to hunker down and hide out for a bit before we emerged with clearer vision.

As well as a refuge, I think I saw the mountains as a sort of gateway. To healing. To a form of remodelling, remaking. Somehow I believed, I hoped, that the heightened anxiety of the past year would retreat slowly into the green, merge vaporous into the fog, be lifted to join the gentle eucalypt haze, a distant, untouchable thing, removed from the day-to-day reality of our present lives. I didn't have a name for my theory—it was more of a feeling than anything else—that if I could find a place safe enough to hide out, eventually, somehow, anxiety would just give up and stop chasing me. Perhaps I don't even need to tell you this by now; you can probably already guess: It didn't all work out quite like this. For one thing, I dramatically underestimated anxiety's persistence.

**

The Blue Mountains themselves had always felt special to me, a place of rest, refreshment, removal. On my thirteenth birthday my parents treated my brother and me to a weekend away in a lodge-style hotel with floor-to-ceiling panoramic windows, and a giant stone fireplace. We watched as the light and shadows moved across the mysterious monoliths in the distance, while we welcomed my entrance to teenage-hood. I remember my stylish European father going up to the bar and asking for a fancy 'mocktail' drink for his daughter as she turned the sharp corner into her teen years, and feeling the corner smoothened with love and attention. On my eighteenth birthday, we stayed once more in the Blue Mountains in a converted monastery, now guest house, amongst hushed, lamplit corners and stone corridors. We invited Katelyn to join us, and she and I shared a room and talked deep into the chilled starlit night. And around seven years later, to mark our first wedding anniversary, Mike and I walked around the mountain edges hand in hand, taking in the new angles and unexpected vistas of a life being fused together. We spent the night in a boutique B&B, with a four-poster bed and private fireplace.

Our rental house was no B&B and definitely no monastery. A basic wooden structure sprawling into a tangled bushland garden, it gave authenticity to the term 'rustic'. But it was set apart, on the edge of a mountain street. To our eyes, at least, it appeared special. And not just our eyes. We received daily visits from wallabies bobbling in the long, dry grass of our garden, and flocks of musical rainbow lorikeets gathered, sometimes competitively, at the birdfeeder on our front veranda. Mike pulled out his guitar, something he had barely done in the last year, and played barefoot on the veranda. Most of all what I remember about that time is the light coming in through the wide, uncovered windows of our sunroom, filtering through the gaps in the gum trees, weaving warmth into our weary hearts, in between the iridescent fibres of friendships being gently retied, and in amongst the chords of Mike's guitar. For three months, we breathed in daily the scent of eucalyptus rising from the forest, we worked side by side, and all the while my body adjusted to its new role as home of a growing human being. I hoped the tiny child growing hidden inside me was as cosy as any mountain hospitality we were receiving.

During our time in the mountains, we started trying out new churches. We settled, for the time being, on a small Presbyterian church a few suburbs and mountain curves down. The drive itself each week was therapeutic. In the small, quaint building with the gentle, accepting crowd of local parishioners, I started again to sing songs of worship, my lips moving in alignment with my heart, to sit through sermons without fear or distraction as I sucked on the packet of lollies I had brought with me, to breathe more slowly as I cradled my growing belly.

It was nearly a perfect picture, but not quite.

The summer heat brought out a strange odour of nicotine and something else, stronger, from the carpet that did nothing for the morning sickness (something of a misnomer) I found hit me quite hard in the evenings. I lay for many hours on the couch, sipping ginger ale and eating only lightly. The nausea gave me an uneasy feeling, even as I reminded myself it was normal. It was hard to break the hardwired associations with anxiety.

And I was vigilant.

Even in the mountains, it seemed, I found it hard to actually, really, truly rest.

With the zeal of a soldier, I patrolled the perimeters of my body, alert for the smallest of changes. Like a woman in battle, I hardly ever switched off, not even when I slept.

***

Now, here is a strange thing. Anxiety doesn't only feed off pain, it can thrive on positives too. Even the most benign event or occurrence can spark it. And the really good things, they can send it into turbo drive. If events like holidays or parties tipped it off, you can only imagine how it was handling the very new and still-ripening news of our pregnancy after such a long interval of waiting and hoping.

While some people might be over-cocky about the future, glasses full to overflowing to the point of water sploshing over the sides, others (like me) tend to keep the glass half-full, in permanent fear of it tipping. The more precious the possibility, the more delicate the glass and its contents. That half-full status can, however, lead to some pretty complex and acrobatic acts of thought experimentation. In case your mind doesn't automatically run on the same rails, or off them as the case may be, I'll try to give you an example of a typical conversation between Mike and me in those days:

Mike: 'I still can't believe it.'

Me: 'I know. Me neither.'

Mike: 'It's the best news all year. It's truly amazing.'

Me: 'It is… But…'

Mike: 'But what?'

Me: 'But what if something goes wrong?'

Mike: 'Like what?'

Me: 'Like anything. Anything that could turn amazing to appalling.'

Mike: 'But why? Why would that happen?'

Me: 'Because it could. Especially in the early days.'

Mike: 'Well, of course it could, but it doesn't mean it *will*, does it?'

Me: 'No. Of course not. But it *could*.'

Mike: 'If something bad is going to happen (which I hope and pray it doesn't), it's going to happen anyway, so why waste time worrying about it?'

Long pause. Sound of swallowing.

Me: 'I guess because if I'm worrying, it means I'm preparing, and that makes me feel less afraid. If I'm ready for the worst, then it can't surprise me as much when it happens.'

Mike: 'That makes no sense.'

Me: 'I know.'

Anxiety: 'I don't always make sense. That's the whole point. And, also, a whole lot of my power.'

***

Though I told no-one, not even Mike, every day, multiple times a day, I checked. Obsessively. Fanatically. I wonder if every new mum does it, or if it was my anxiousness that made me more vigilant? The fact that good news had visited us after so long seemed *too* good to be true. Like any well-trained worrier, I fretted about each and every *what if*. A heavy line of apprehension hung beneath everything I did. I knew no pregnancy was one hundred percent secure, especially in the first ten weeks, and I'd heard (and tried not to read) so many stories of what could go wrong. We'd shared our good news very early; perhaps this is common with IVF, as everyone is already praying and watching for you. It is hard not to give the verdict out when it comes in. But the openness gave it extra vulnerability. We didn't yet know if we would be able to get pregnant again or if this was it. What if this was our one chance, and we lost it? Each time I went to the toilet, I feared for a few seconds what I would see.

And for eleven weeks, everything was just as it should be. At last, even I began to think that just maybe, things would turn out okay after all.

***

Around a month into our mountains stay we had visitors in the form of my old friend Jane and her family. It was just on the eleventh week of our pregnancy, and we'd had a positive scan a week before at the local IVF clinic. Jane, always generous, brought gifts. While we unwrapped the paper, revealing a bright, wooden baby present, we tossed the newly discovered joy of our pregnancy back and forth like the bouquet at a wedding, tied together with laughter and stories. Our friends had struggled with us; now they could share in our celebration. It felt good to see our own relief mirrored on their faces.

After Jane and the others left later that day, Mike and I decided to take a drive down the mountain to Wentworth Falls Lake for a gentle walk and to take some time to chat, away from our books. While much of the mountain landscape is the rough Australian beauty of green-grey trees and granite rocks, the sort of intrepid landscape bushwalkers and explorers can and do get lost in, the lake gave the appearance of a more refined gentility. The type of place where ducks choose to bob unhurriedly, where people walk in gentle circles, and where everything is, on the whole, hushed and quietened.

We, however, were not quiet. In body or minds. Though we lay down on a picnic blanket and faced one another intimately as we talked, we were far from relaxed. Our subject of discussion was the future, with a capital F—specifically, finances. We'd come home, or at least in the near vicinity. But how did we make the next year, the next six months even, work? Mike had left his job suddenly, and although he had found temporary teaching work back at the University of New South Wales, was it enough? Did I need to find a job too? Not just for the immediate term, but for the longer view. We were, after all, about to become parents. Life was about to change, and one of those changes would surely mean it would cost more. Maybe I should retrain, we thought. My PhD in English literature, which I was at that point hardly halfway through, was no guarantee of future employment. The academic track, it is well known, is far from stable. Even more precarious, my real interest was in writing, a career path in Australia that I knew only a miniscule part of the population could rely on as their sole income.

We needed to be realistic, we said solemnly as we faced one another from our side-by-side reclining position. We needed to put down practical tent-peg roots as well as emotional ones. And yet the timing seemed all off. I was frustrated. We both were.

'I don't know why we have to talk about this now!' I said, standing hurriedly. For a moment I faced the still, translucent waters of the lake. Over on a small wooden bridge, a family stopped to look below them, into the shallows. A little boy and girl hopped forward over an inviting pattern of rocks. And I felt it come, warm and sudden. For a moment I thought, with shock, that I had wet myself. But of course, that wasn't the real horror.

With all my fears perched on my shoulders like squawking magpies, I wasted no time racing to the car, and from the barely private front seat I leant over to check. Our blank slate future was suddenly tainted red.

I heard myself let out something like a guttural howl. A cry. A lakeside lament. Mike climbed in beside me and with the larger, shaking hands of father-in-waiting, of husband-rendered helpless, he started the car before we knew yet where to drive.

I typed Jane's name into my phone and pressed call. My friend who'd smiled nonstop at us just that morning was also a medical doctor. She delivered precise doctor's instructions on what to do next. 'Go home, pack a bag, be calm.'

Then we drove down the mountain.

Of course, we could have waited or gone to the local hospital, but it was the weekend and Jane had told us they wouldn't be able to do any scans there. We wanted answers. I needed to know. The spectacular, spiralling mountain views were the backdrop to the twisting, downward spiral of my thoughts.

As we drove, I rang several friends whose voices talked some reserves of calmness into me, even as I leaked it out. They had also had bleeding, they said, at various points in their pregnancies. It didn't have to mean the worst; it could be nothing, they said. 'But it could be something, too, right?' I said. It could, they conceded, and said they would pray. Bec offered us a bed at her house should we need it, and she also carried some crucial information. Her friend was a midwife at the Sydney hospital nearest to our families. She had spoken to her. They did scans on the weekend. Still without certainty of being seen, we decided to give the hospital a try.

The admitting nurse at the hospital looked at us with efficient compassion as we gave our reason for coming, as we attempted to fill out the formal contours of my condition.

I made the mistake of using the bathroom, and then had to lie still in a hospital bed and wait as they pumped my bladder full again. Mike sat at the end of the bed, his back to the privacy curtain, and I half dozed, hungry and still nauseous from my upside-down morning sickness. And we waited.

Sometime around 12 am, a kind man in scrubs wheeled us into a large, quiet room. The ultrasound machine sat in the corner, still and blinking, like a royal chief, waiting to declare our future. Mike squeezed my hand. We made silent eye contact. One way or another, we were about to find out what would happen next. The ultrasound technician waved the sticky wand across my stomach in gentle, unrushed circles. There was an excruciating moment of pause, like a long swim under water, breath held to bursting.

And then, 'There she is,' he smiled at us at last. 'Can you see her dancing?'

The world simultaneously narrowed and expanded. My worst fear had happened, and it hadn't. As our baby somersaulted on the screen, my heart quietened, bobbed in my chest gently, like the ducks on the water, like my baby in the watery casing of my womb. For a few minutes, life shone bright and luminous. Mine. And hers.

God's gift was before us, and it was entirely beyond our control. Again. And once more, it could have gone either way, and not one ounce of my worrying would have done anything to tip the compass even a millimetre.

It was a frightening thought, yes. But it was also a liberating one.

It wasn't a miscarriage after all, but a burst blood vessel. A tiny, hidden part of me gone haywire, setting off a whole string of unpredicted results. Even I hadn't prepared for—or even imagined—that.

That night, relief and gratitude came alongside me, breathing deep, cupped around my middle, tenderly, like the soft covers of my parents' bed, which they had given up for us on our return from hospital. And in the morning when I awoke, we made a decision. We decided that perhaps it was time to move on down from the mountains, from our temporary hideout, to find somewhere more permanent to settle in Sydney, closer to family and friends and twenty-four-hour scanning machines.

Despite my ineptitude at anything geometric or mathematical, I was beginning to see a pattern. Whenever significant life events or changes occurred, fear followed closely after them. And my usual response was to try and get away from it as far and as fast as possible. For whatever reason, anxiety loves movement. Maybe it thinks if it can just keep you in motion, keep you trying to elude it, through running and weaving and dodging, it will never be caught. Except, it doesn't work. I saw that now.

It only makes you tired. It weighs you down.

Perhaps it was the new life taking root inside me, perhaps it was my own instinct, perhaps it was God; but this time, as fear nipped at my heels, I didn't want to run, or hide.

I wanted to build. I wanted to surround myself in support. I wanted to put down roots. I wanted to grow.

And at the end of the day, more than anything else, I just wanted to be able to stand.

Chapter Nineteen

Seeds of Growth

Our new street in Sydney was called, appropriately, Nursery Street. Our latest rental abode was a tiny, neat, two-storey townhouse that would have looked just right nestled within the pages of a children's picture book. A builder friend of ours at the time commented that everything had been constructed just a little smaller than average. The stairs, the doorframes, the rooms. One Saturday afternoon we had our friends Nick and Katy over for lunch. Nick is the only person I know who manages to make Mike appear small beside him. We sat down at the table like giants playing tea parties in a dollhouse.

If the house was small, life itself felt larger than ever. I was so aware of every sensation in those days, as if the new body within me woke me up. I felt the spring breeze rushing through the upstairs windows, brushing across me as I unpacked and nested, as I typed of a morning on my dissertation, eager to accelerate my progress before *she* joined us. And yes, she was a she; we knew that much for sure. Did we want to know the gender of our baby, or be surprised, the ultrasound technician had asked at our nineteen-week scan. We had had more than enough surprises we told her, not even needing to look at one another to affirm our answer. We wanted to know.

She had a nose like a tiny ski jump, and a perfectly shaped head, we told our families as we gathered around the screen to watch the DVD of the ultrasound together. We were living each moment of this first, miracle pregnancy in high definition, in slow motion.

While I worked facing out at a window from a desk in the nursery, one that we would move out and replace with a white, wooden cot when the time was right, Mike's office was a room in the ceiling, a secret hideout accessed only by a pull-down ladder. As my belly grew, I could no longer fit in the narrow hallway when the ladder was down. Our baby was asserting its space in our lives.

In keeping with the tiny house theme, our backyard was little more than a postage stamp imprint of ground. A tiny square, literally a pile of discarded dirt and tangled overgrowth when we arrived, it was in serious need of love. Of TLC. Mike's parents came over to help us tend to the miniature jungle. With faithful grandparent-to-be ferocity, they pulled out weeds and smoothed the dirt, preparing the neglected soil for growth. In the wake of their labour, with a tender reverence, Mike sprinkled grass seeds across our tiny patch of prepared earth. With gentle hands he watered it. And then, once more, we waited. Admittedly, our waiting was less of the patient and more of the expectant-eager variety. We paced outside in the still, cool of night with torches outstretched as we knelt down and carefully surveyed our little seeds. We were starting over, and we were beginning small. And each new hint of movement mattered.

Some people practise their future parenting movements on a pet; a dog in particular seems to work well. We tended grass. As the blades appeared, bit by victorious bit, we exclaimed to one another, 'Look, look, it's getting so much taller!' When it rained, we watched from the living room window, concerned. Was it tough enough yet to handle so much impact? Could we somehow protect it? Our devotion to our sprouting seedlings lasted for as long as we waited and prepared for the revelation of the hidden form within me.

***

During that time of waiting, several other seeds were planted. We renewed old friendships, visited churches, and I started teaching a community creative writing class where each Wednesday night I met with an odd, eclectic bunch of mostly older folks who fed me parenting anecdotes and advice, as I helped them find their words on paper.

Their advice was only the tip of the iceberg of what I was taking in.

Along with my thesis and teaching job, I was working hard in other areas of my life too: namely my role as new-mum-to-be. As I looked around me at my friends, at the flood of information, mostly well-intended, on parenting, from blogs, to books, to a plethora of competing training courses, all promising to teach you the *best* skills and methods for parenting success, I started to draw pictures in my head of what a good mum was, of the sort of mum I wanted to be.

Always the keen student, I began making lists, both internal and external, and ticking them off as I went. I studiously collected and read the recommended manuals on pregnancy and birth and breastfeeding. I attended the prenatal classes and practised putting nappies on dummies and dolls, and I talked to friends to fill in any gaps they left out or that were unclear. I took the vitamins with extra folate and ate my fibre and attended every one of my medical appointments on time. These lists were all understandable and even, mostly, beneficial. But there were other lists I made. Mental lists that came from nowhere else but inside me. Ones I didn't read in books but knew about all too well.

Now that I was about to have a baby, I told myself, there were more things than the physical ones that needed to change. *I* needed to change. I needed to fix anything that wasn't good enough to be part of a new mum, and I had only months left to do it. Forefront of my internal priorities, unsurprisingly, was my battle with anxiety and its messy manifestations. If I was going to be ready for this baby, I told myself with the authority of some sort of all-knowing parenting-guru, then anxiety needed to go.

In an effort to declutter all the areas I thought needed to be cleaned up before I was ready to bring our baby home in her government-approved, multi-anchored car seat, the tyranny of *shoulds* came marching back in, not so much as goals but as stern slaps over the back of my soon-to-be-baby-holding hands. I *should* have finished my PhD by now, so that I could give my undivided attention to the baby; I *should* have learnt to drive so I didn't have to rely on other people; I *should* have chosen a practical career before now, one that would actually, you know, maybe help us buy a house one day that had a garden bigger than two metres square. And perhaps the strongest *should* of all, the one that overarched them all and filled me with guilt if I stopped too long to think about it—the holy should. The one that whisper-shouted in a voice that seemed to carry extra spiritual authority, even as it was my own: You *should* have overcome these things by now. If your faith was stronger, you *would* have.

It was in the middle of all this, as I bustled and prepared, worked and worried, that PD cleared its throat harshly and barged its way back in. With a glaring absence of manners, it filled the tiny dollhouse of a home with its jittery presence. I wonder if the new blades of grass felt it, the disturbance in the air. It was a surprise to meet again under such circumstances; and, of course, it wasn't. In that sweet little house of promise, my physical sensations of anxiety returned, my painful stomach, my restless thoughts. After one hard afternoon spent walking the hilly, busy streets of our neighbourhood, trying, and failing, to beat the anxiety from my system through my feet and into the pavement, to release the tension that was building inside me like a load of rocks, Mike stood close behind me and told me what I already knew but needed to hear.

'You need to talk to someone,' he said. 'How about I make a phone call?'

During our time in Melbourne, as I already said, we had stayed in touch with the Wise Woman. She told us that an old colleague of hers just *happened to* have started working out of offices within easy walking distance of Nursery Street. As we prepared to hold new, pulsing, hopeful life in our arms, the Wise Man around the corner helped me, at last, to let some other unnecessary weight go from my back.

Chapter Twenty

Letting Go of Holy Shoulds

On the eve of my grand entrance onto the stage of motherhood, I had but one motive as I walked into the small, nondescript office of my newest psychologist in the suburbs: to bring the enemy anxiety down, once and for all. As if I were a contestant on an emotional weight-loss challenge, I had my goal firmly in mind. I would have had no problem describing it in vivid detail. I wanted to emerge a better, stronger, leaner version of myself.

One good enough to deserve this new life inside me.

I arrived at the small waiting room at the top of a flight of concrete stairs out of breath and in need of a glass of water. The kindly receptionist, who also, it turned out, was the Wise Man's wife, offered me one with an understanding smile, her eyes warm on my belly, and I drank deeply.

Where the Wise Woman had been a dancer in her spare time, the Wise Man was a surfer. I saw the ebbing rhythms of the sea in his languid movements, in the measured ease of his pace, as he appeared in the waiting room and directed me to his office. I found my seat on the centre of the couch and leant forward in nervous anticipation. I had become so accustomed to sitting on these couches over the years, it was almost like muscle memory kicked in, and I assumed my position of alert readiness. The Wise Man rocked backwards a few times on his chair, in a way that reminded me of a relaxed schoolboy.

'So, Nikki,' he said, in his disarmingly casual way, the slow drawl of an accent as Australian as summer sun on rocks. 'What's been going on?'

I told him how my anxiety, how GAD, and in particular PD, had returned once more, like some sort of dirty thief sneaking in during the night and messing up my neat house, trampling over every room, even the baby nursery with the small pool of golden lamplight and the mobile perched over the bassinet with the music set to the tune of serenity. I filled him in on the various contours of my story, the peaks and the many troughs, summing it all up finally, like a chief defendant in my own case, my emotional fitness the topic of interrogation. 'I should be better now,' I proclaimed loudly. 'I mean, I'm going to be a mother.' I pointed at my protruding stomach, as if it were obvious that the picture sitting before him was all completely wrong.

The Wise Man sipped his coffee cup infuriatingly slowly, all the while studying me with calm eyes beneath glasses tipped down on his nose. He was clearly not in a hurry. If my life were an ocean, and words were waves that would carry me safely to shore, he was prepared to wait until the right ones arrived. I was ready to slide into shore as fast as possible. I wanted to win peace and take it home with me like some sort of surfing trophy or carnival game prize, shiny and bright and oversized in my arms.

Thankfully, the Wise Man had by then years of experience with stories like mine, of spiritual perfectionist stilt-walkers wobbling into his office, and his ear was good, even over the clamour of my own attempts to explain. He read between the words I spoke, ramshackle and breathless, like so many train carriages banging together, careening down a hill. Alongside the fear in my voice, he heard something else. Perhaps he even saw it too. While in my belly I brought in with me the hope of growing new life, behind me I dragged the heavy deadweight of years of self-condemnation.

It wasn't just PD messing with my future. It was me.

When he spoke at last, it was in the form of a quiet question, much like the Wise Woman had begun our journey. 'Why all the *shoulds*, Nikki?' he said on almost a sigh, a shrug in his voice. 'Why *should* you be better by now. What do you think?' He sipped his coffee again and waited.

'Well, because I'm a Christian, of course!' I burst out quickly on top of his words, as if it were the most self-evident thing in the world.

I talked on, quoting the Bible at the Wise Man like missiles I sent across the space between us. I knew he was a believer himself; he often spoke at churches and had even written a book that included discussion of Jesus' approach to busyness and stress. I'd read it, but perhaps I'd forgotten the message it contained, or not understood it. I thought he'd be on my side. I filed through all the passages I knew about anxiety and worry, everything I could think of, and hurled them into the air across the room at him, like scrunched up pieces of paper, tests I'd failed, and attempted with the force of them to stop the rocking of his chair in its tracks. *Do not worry, trust in God, perfect love drives out fear,* each another mark against me, evidence of my always erring, of my need for urgent repair, of my fear and lack of faith.

'Can a Christian not feel unpleasant emotions?' he answered, this time a little more animated, as he warmed up to his topic. 'Do you think the disciples never felt fear? The prophets never experienced nerves?'

He began to quote the Bible back at me, less aggressively than I had done, but no less solidly. Actually, he told me stories, one of the best languages I know for conveying truth. He told me about all the failed heroes, stumbling disciples and used-by-God messes that populated the pages of my favourite, but not uncomplicated, book. His words were engaging and catching as he took his time to catalogue the high maintenance, dysfunctional, up and down crowd of God's people. There was Paul, evangelist to the gentiles, who stumbled often as he spoke, bold on the page, but not in person, who once required a blinding light to take off his blinkers and get his attention. There was Peter, who denied his Saviour not one but three times, while he warmed his hands by a fire in his Lord's darkest hour, but who nonetheless carried on to become the Rock. There was Moses, God's man for the job of leading his chosen nation out of slavery, who stuttered so much that he needed his brother, Aaron, to speak for him. Then, of course, there was King David, who wrote the psalms with a poet's high sensitivity but committed catastrophic blunders worthy of B-grade soap operas. And who afterwards sank into sorrow, into a pit of despair, perhaps even into depression.

All of these, the Wise Man told me, feared, and trembled, and fell down; but did this make them any less loved, any less cared for by God? If anything, the inverse was true. They were all, in different ways, powerfully used.

But at the same time, they experienced powerful emotions.

What were the psalms of lament but God not only permitting but giving us the very language, the building block of words, to describe the darkness of this life, the Wise Man challenged me, offered me, *counselled* me.

But even then, he wasn't finished. He waited while I took a sip of water, taking it all in.

'And what about Jesus?' he said at last.

'Did Jesus feel anxiety?' I said, a little dismayed at the possible act of irreverence we were communally committing.

'Did he? You tell me?'

'Well, he was perfect,' I exclaimed.

'Yes.'

'So…'

'What about the tears?' The Wise Man spoke the words across the room and this time he had the missile. It was powerful.

I hadn't thought about the tears, or if I had, never quite like this. 'Jesus cried when he saw Mary and Martha's grief at losing their brother,' I said aloud, letting the words take root inside me, picturing it. A double dose of sisterly sorrow, shared by the Saviour.

He didn't just cry in that moment.

Jesus wept.

Loudly. Passionately. Violently.

Apparently 'wept' isn't even a forceful enough word to encapsulate Jesus' outpouring at that moment. Translators describe it as something beyond even sobbing, something as visceral as snorting.

And again, the night before his crucifixion, in the garden, he cried, his tears mixed with blood.

'With blood,' the Wise Man emphasised. 'Those were no ordinary tears.'

Jesus might not have experienced GAD or PD, but he definitely felt anguish, mental pain, dark emotions. He allowed himself to feel things. And he let his feelings out. In tears. In weeping. In blood. Sorrow to the point of death. Because some things are worthy of tears. Even the tears of God in flesh.

'Do you think anxiety is sin?' the Wise Man asked me, no longer rocking, this time leaning in close.

'I don't know.'

He paused. I thought. I thought about Jesus again. And about the pain. And about the tears. I thought about brokenness, and I thought about healing. I thought about the cross.

Jesus inhabited a body like mine, without sin, yes, but not without dread, alarm, pain and foreboding. So…

'No, I don't think so,' I answered at last.

'It's not your fault, Nikki,' the Wise Man said, gently but firmly. 'And you are not on trial. You are not in trouble.'

And then, the moment I believe I turned a corner, the moment my interior view shifted from a small, confined room to a wide, deep sky.

'It's time,' the Wise Man spoke to me. 'Time to walk off the battlefield. Time to lay down your weapons. There's no need to fight anymore.'

I thought about all the times I had attempted to conquer anxiety by fighting it. Sometimes literally taking my fists to it. I remembered one chill night in Melbourne, when my adrenaline went through the roof in our apartment, and my husband held up his larger hands and allowed me to hit against them. Punch after punch, as hard as I could.

'I hate you, anxiety!' I had yelled, through tears, as I made my knuckles ache with the impact. 'I hate you so much. Go away, go away. Go away.' I'd punched and punched and punched. And in the end, I'd collapsed, not in relief, but exhaustion.

Fighting wasn't just ineffective, it was draining, emptying. If I wanted to be full, emptying myself of anxiety wasn't the answer after all.

The Wise Man was right. I had stopped running, but I hadn't stopped fighting, trying so hard to triumph that I was falling flat on my face. How could I have got it so wrong, mistaking striving for growth?

A time not to strive, but to abide.

The Wise Man wasn't saying anything new; not all of it, anyway. But in that time and place, somehow it spoke more clearly than ever before. Like a sword of peace, to my embattled heart.

'There's more to you than your anxiety, Nikki,' he said. 'You are not defined by it.'

> *It's time to stop battling.*
> *It's time to stop trying to be perfect. Even in your expectations of your capacity for faith.*
> *It's time to trust in Jesus, not yourself.*
> *Because it is finished.*
> *And because it is finished, even on those days when you feel anxiety baring its teeth and opening its jaws to roar—and you will again—you don't need to despair.*
> *To fight, or to flee.*
> *You just need to abide.*

God was capable of holding all of me, even the parts I felt most ashamed of. The words 'do not worry' were not to be read so much as an admonition but as an encouragement. I didn't need to be a perfectly assembled model of womanhood to be a mum, or a perfect, non-cracked human to be whole. I just needed to trust that in Jesus, I was loved.

'Go gently.'

Those were the words I heard the Wise Man say at the end of each session, to me and others, again and again, because no-one can hear them enough. It was a unique way to say goodbye, to close a conversation, but I suppose in that office he'd learnt over the years just how much it needed to be said.

When we learn to go gently, we walk within the bounds of where we've been designed to walk; we exercise compassion on ourselves and on others. We walk in grace. While restraints and limitations on our capacities can feel like losses, they can, in fact, be soft strengths. Remembering our humanness can be a comfort, an encouragement to look to the divine. To find our centre. Jars of clay who don't think the jar is meant to be the treasure.

I walked out of the office of the Wise Man and back onto the suburban roads, busy at peak hour. At sunset. Cars buzzed, trains clattered on their tracks, pedestrians rushed past. It was all the same, but it was different too. I recall it as a moment of illumination. I might not have been blinded and re-visioned, Paul-like, but there *was* light. More of it than usual. Or at least of a different quality. And it opened my eyes. I saw the orange-gold glint on the train tracks and in the headlights of the cars heading home. All around me I saw it. I could feel it within me, too.

I walked out of the Wise Man's office not better, but lighter.

Chapter Twenty-One

So Much Bigger

I am learning that God is so much bigger than what we know here...
Hang in there, kid, and know that Jesus travels with you always.

—GVDK, in a letter, 1997.

Is it possible, perhaps without even knowing it—and this is the strangest part of all—that while he was alive, my brother was preparing me, preparing us all, for the time he would leave us? Were his words, written and spoken in the present, actually intended as gifts that he would leave behind for us, messages in bottles for the time I, and others, would need them most? My mother once described my brother's faith as being 'so quiet that it spoke so loud'. Perhaps this is why his words still follow me, even now. Whispers, in the end, last much longer than shouts.

Several conversations I had with my brother over the years stand out in my memory. It's like I can still recall not just the content of them, but the mood too. I can still feel their impact, the imprint of the lessons learnt pressed into the holey places in my heart.

I remember one day, shortly after I began following Jesus, I was lying on one of the old couches upstairs in the family room in the rental house we lived in at the time. Once a good piece of furniture, neatly stitched and upright, age and constant wear had taken its toll. Though its body was still sturdy, the arms of the couch were badly torn. Part of the blame can be laid on Sparky, the family cat, who had an almost obsessive need to scratch at things. In a similar way he'd wrecked the interior of my mum's car. Thanks to his efforts, the couch's once plump arms now puckered, like an old person who'd spent too many youthful years at the beach and whose skin had started to sag and bunch in strange ways. Through the rips, you could see its bare foam innards, seeping out. Mum hated that couch and had sent it upstairs mostly to keep it out of sight. But I loved it. It was ordinary and comfy, without any pretension. Its steadfast solidity always welcomed me. I knew at its core that it held me.

As I lay there in the summer heat under the ceiling fan, falling against the foam after a long day at school, Greg breezed in and paused for a moment to talk to me. I was always glad when he took the time to notice me in his latter teen years. Between his friends, his own study, church, and all his other commitments, our dedicated time together was becoming rarer and rarer. I listened eagerly as he began to speak, and it became quickly apparent he had a lot to let out. He'd just been to a Bible study where they'd been unpacking some tough questions, and Greg was brimming over with ideas and implications. All the stuff that didn't fit neatly into our new faith tumbled out of his mouth in a cacophony of words, like *where did dinosaurs fit into the Bible? Why did a good God allow suffering? Where had sin come from, anyway? Was the apple really an apple?* I hadn't thought of it all, not yet. I was a new baby believer, mouth wide open to receive scoops of information, as much and as solid as I could, but I was still learning how to chew and digest. As his questions and musings kept going in so many different directions, they actually began to scare me a little. How could there be any certainty when there was still so much we couldn't understand?

'It's all so big,' I said finally when he paused.

'I know,' he replied.

But unlike me, I could clearly see that my brother wasn't scared. Not even a bit. If anything, he was excited, invigorated by all his mental explorations, curious and open. His blue eyes gleamed with new discovery, just like they used to when we were kids, and he mastered a new LEGO project.

Years later, when I was overseas in Europe on that final trip before he would leave us, my brother wrote me a letter. At the time, I thought it was written only for the situation I found myself in, so far from home:

Don't be afraid in the face of a world that seems big.

Jesus is bigger still

He travels with you always.

Love eternally, Greg

He always signed his letters and cards that way. 'Eternally.' Then, we must have brushed over it, but after, and now, it has come to mean so much more.

My brother was comfortable with big things: he loved astronomy and the idea of a galactic-sized universe; he loved philosophy and poetry and all the murky, effervescent edges of things. Though not messy himself, he was never put out by the mess of others. He didn't back away from things, or people, that didn't fit in neat moulds, that couldn't be crammed into square boxes. He was the friend everyone went to with their broken hearts, knowing that he would cradle the pieces tenderly.

My brother trusted God like I trusted the old couch. Even when things began to change, when stuff spilled out, or over, he knew the foundation was solid, reliable, true, and he sank right into it. He could afford to share space with the questions, even the seemingly unanswerable ones, and to suffer some chaos, when he knew the core was reliable. And not just reliable, but made of the most precious materials of all: grace, mercy, steadfast love.

And he lived into it.

After he left us, and suffering was no longer just a contained, bordered theological problem but a ravaging flood, I clung to his words. And as often as I could, I tried to lean back into the solidity of the God behind it all that I knew to be true, even when I struggled to feel it amidst all the questions.

***

I sometimes wonder how my brother had the insight he did so young. So soon. So strong. It was like he had an X-ray power, a capacity to see to the heart of things that the rest of us didn't have. The suburb we grew up in was clean and tidy, at least on the outside. Greg went to a private school, he was popular, he had good friends, an excellent education, and parents, not to mention a little sister, who loved him inside out. And yet he knew; somehow, he knew. Life wasn't always what it appeared to be. Beneath the smoothest of exteriors was a buzzing world of brokenness. Broken hearts. Broken connections. Broken bodies. How was he, so young and inexperienced, already so able to spot the cracks? I've spent a lot of years wondering, and my only answer is this: it was a gift. My brother had been given a gift. His life was a gift. My brother himself was a gift. And he was given. To us all.

The more years that go by, it seems less like he has departed and more like he has simply gone ahead, taking the first steps like he always did, leading the way and waiting for us to follow. And would you believe it, even now, I still feel like I am trying to catch up. The younger child always a few steps behind, straining ahead, following the elder brother home. And I'm so thankful that he's ahead of me. Eternally.

***

What if there is something wrong with me?

Those were the last meaningful words I spoke to my brother. Not the hurried, angry final-ever words at the door as we were caught in the midst of a temporary squabble. Though for a time I worried over these, I see them now as fleeting, largely insignificant. I mean the last *real* words. Our last genuine conversation. Thoughts delivered from my heart to his and back again along the shared channels of sibling understanding that we had been travelling since childhood.

Though I usually found my way to my brother's room to emotionally unload, on this occasion, I remember being too upset to even journey across the hallway. As my older brother sat beside me on my bed with the white and blue doona cover dappled with yellow daisies, I confessed to him the question I feared most of all. While I did not yet have a name for it, while it had not yet jumped out from behind the curtains and shouted *boo!*, I can see now that anxiety was waiting in the wings even then, peaking out every so often under pressure and blowing hot air on my neck. I felt things deeply. I missed my family in Holland. I wasn't yet sure of my new place in Sydney. I was scared of the future. I was overly shy. Uncertain. I had deep, hidden, underwater currents of fears I couldn't even yet articulate.

Greg studied me in his calm, unhurried way, tracing slow circles on the printed daisies.

'Everyone has something,' he said at last. 'Even people who don't look like they do. Life isn't a straight line. It's more of a curve. And we are all standing somewhere along it. We are all struggling, in some way. None of us is ever perfectly secure.'

Essentially, after just twenty-two years, he already had it figured out earth side. No-one is perfect, not one. Everyone has gaps, holes, uneven inconsistencies. Every single person needs filling with something bigger and better than themselves.

While I had been in Europe, Greg had been deeply affected by some of the material he had been reading, specifically the books of Brennan Manning, who wrote a passionate message of God's love, God's fondness, for his 'ragamuffin' people, and the unbridled, radical lyrics of musician Rich Mullins, who was to die tragically in a car accident just a year earlier than Greg.

Greg mourned his death.

And Greg wrote to me, from across the waters, about God's love for every ragamuffin, about his amazing grace that covered over all. Not fake, theoretical, prettied-up, only-on-Sunday grace, but gritty, real, huge, all-encompassing love. A love that my brother himself seemed to be bathing in like never before in those last few months of his life on earth; a pool of God's tender acceptance, so sweet and so true that it made him want to share it around. To throw it, like a lifeline, to his sister across the oceans.

That last letter, that final conversation, I believe my brother was trying to tell me something lasting. Though his tone was, as it always was, quiet, steady, humorous even, I see now that he was calling it from his full soul across the chasm to mine, across and through and into my deepest places where Jesus lived and anxiety visited.

You don't need to be perfect.

You just need to remember that you are perfectly loved.

And his last words in that last letter, across space and across time: *Hang in there.*

Or like our friend Pilgrim once said, let it dangle.

Or in the words of our Father, 'Be still, and know that I am God!' (Ps 46:10).

Chapter Twenty-Two

Good Surprises

There are lots of things I'd like to tell my brother today if only I had the chance. The stuff I never got to say, not loud enough anyway, not with the emphasis I'd give it now. Like, thank you. For everything. And, you were right. About most things. And, sorry, but in hindsight the 1990s earring was never a good idea.

But even more than words, I sometimes wish I could just have him with me for one more day. And I would show him what came after, and alongside. After the loss, alongside the pain, something else emerged: Joy. Hope. Life.

I'd tell him some new stories too. Like this one:

For two chronically late individuals like my husband and I, it was a surprise to find that our first child came early. One midwinter evening, I swayed back and forth through early contractions while Mike typed on his keyboard beside me, giving last birth pushes to his own creative work of a dissertation. We drove to the hospital in the middle of the night, shouting at red lights, laughing at the towels wedged beneath my legs, wide eyed with anticipation and the unknown. After we waddled into the hospital, I laboured through the night, through pained laughter and exhausted tears, and when at last she travelled down the birth canal to meet us, she got lost on the way. And it didn't surprise me at all. We named her Evangeline Grace, bringer of good news, because that's what she was.

Less than two years later, our first son was born. We named him Willem Gregory, giving him my brother's name wedged like a rock of remembrance in the middle of his own, and today, at seven years old, he loves LEGO and thinks and talks like someone ten years above his age. Coincidence? I think not.

We thought we were done. But less than two years after that came the biggest plot twist of all, the child we never expected or planned for. It was almost like God decided to prank us, and as initial shock turned to laughter, we opened our palms to receive him. Joseph Michael, meaning God gives even more, arrived almost despite us, without any of the perceived power of our personal worrying or even prayer. It seems God is sometimes into the idea of spontaneous surprise parties. Even the less-than-half-a-percent-chance type.

This book, then, has told of the first twelve years of my journey with anxiety, beginning with the event of my brother's death and culminating with these stories of new life. I finish here, however, not because this is the point grand closure was reached and nothing worth telling ever happened again: *and then we became parents and retreated to our cosy world of family and lived happily ever after in a permanent filter of undiluted domestic joy.* If you believe that after all you have read, then I clearly haven't told this story well. No, I finish here because I think the next chapter deserves its own story in its own right. Perhaps in time, I will be ready to tell it.

While becoming a parent has remade me, and moulded me in ways beyond telling, it did not cure or banish my anxiety. If anything, a new journey began in that first delivery room, packed full of new challenges and blessings. I read somewhere recently that parenting is, in its essence, a state of uncertainty and vulnerability. It brings with it more questions than answers, as your heart becomes strapped to that of another (or that of three others). Suffice to say, like marriage, like life, parenthood is not an elixir but a relationship. The propensity as a parent to beat yourself up is almost universal. But it is also a time to rest on the arm of our heavenly Father perhaps like few others.

One thing parents come to discover very quickly—we love our children. Desperately, furiously, without end, without bounds. No matter what they do, or how they feel, or even what they cannot say.

A little bit like the Father loves us.

***

As I write this, it is 2020. Two decades across and into the millennium. The year no-one expected. Not even those of us with wild and dreadful imaginations could have predicted this: raging, furious bushfires eating up our land and a pandemic of global proportions squeezing the air from us all. Masks and stay-at-home orders, and tests, and vaccines, and fear everywhere. Anxiety is a word on everyone's tongue now, even those who have never paid it any attention before. As the deaths rise and the restrictions increase, so does the number of people suffering mentally. The world is exposed as a fragile thing, interconnected and vulnerable.

But our communal weakness does more than just shut us out from one another; it opens us up, too. As we close our doors, we have the chance to simultaneously open our lives to one another in new ways. Technology, for all its faults, becomes part of the glue of our new social and emotional fabric. We attend virtual concerts, virtual art tours, and even virtual church services. It is a time to gather, even as we separate.

And amongst all the meet-ups, I stumble on an unexpected but not unwelcome reunion. In 2020, from my computer screen on our kitchen bench, I return to the scene of the Christian campfires of my youth.

It begins when Jodie starts the group on Facebook for those who attended our church in the early days. The group grows quickly to over three hundred members in just a few days. The desire to connect and reminisce is strong. As the photos and memories flood in, many of them including my brother, as members type in their comments from across the globe and closer to home, momentum grows. But it seems we want more. What better way to remember and to draw strength in this time than at a campfire? A time and place is proposed and organised, and word spreads.

It is held in the building of the small, South Coast church of Jamberoo where Jodie now works. Jodie and Graham stand at the front of the building with little more than their acoustic guitars and voices. The rest of us join in from behind the walls of our screens.

And as they begin to play songs on request, old favourites like 'Sing Hallelujah' and 'Be Bold', I watch the names of those joining pop up on the screen, some of whom I have not seen nor heard of for two decades. Conversations and questions sprout spontaneously. Where have you been? How are you going? Two decades of journeys converge in this strange climate of global crisis. Hardly a story is free from some, or multiple, forms of suffering.

But still we sing. Separately. Together. To each other. To the world. There is, of course, no longer any actual campfire, no flames reaching high up close to the trees, cheered on by eager teenagers without fear, no bag of marshmallows or mugs of cocoa, no logs, scratchy but secure against our backs.

We are a long way from home.

Each alone in their own space.

But it doesn't matter.

It was never about the campfire. It wasn't even about the momentary safety we felt in the circle. It was about something much deeper, wider, better. It was about the God we glimpsed then and see now with older, more wide-open eyes. The God large enough to hold all our stories, no matter how big the circle grows, or how far we travel, or how hard it gets.

The God who meets us in the shadows as much as in the glow.

Outside the camp.

Inside our hearts.

Epilogue

Aching Beauty and the Gifts of Anxiety

I've spent a lot of my life not just experiencing anxiety but apologising for it too. For its existence. For its persistence. For the things it has stopped me doing and the way it has made me act. For what it says about me, and about me and God.

I've apologised to Mike, multiple times. 'I'm sorry. I'm so sorry. You shouldn't have to deal with this.' I've said it against his chest, and to his face, and over the phone, and into my hands, tears streaming and heaving, wishing so hard it wasn't this way, that he could have had a happier, easier, more functional wife and life. Or at least one who could cook better, without burning things. Without crumbling so often when she herself felt burnt.

I've apologised to my parents, sometimes to their faces, but most of all inside my head. *I'm sorry I couldn't have been a better child, sunnier, stabler, less shadow and more light.* I'm not sure if even now I've fully shed the weight of being the one left behind. Or if the question will ever be resolved: why me?

I've apologised to God. I'm sorry for my fear. For my heaviness. You offer me peace and I hand back only broken pieces. I'm sorry I don't represent you better to the world. That I can't shine brighter and more often. As if I'm some sort of product ambassador for Christianity who forgot to polish her exterior enough.

I've apologised to the self I think sometimes I should have/could have been. I'm sorry things didn't work out differently. I'm sorry for all the opportunities you've missed because of fear, for all the days and nights of pain when you could have been so much better.

There's no doubt about it. Anxiety ate a whole lot of holes out of my life. It still does, at times. It is the thorn in my side. The sort the apostle Paul admitted to possessing. At first, he asked for it to go, over and over again. Perhaps he even begged.

Until he began to see something else: that weakness could itself be a vessel.

I've prayed for my anxiety to leave me, for me to leave it. I've tried to outsmart it, outrun it, to fight it out. But it remains, and like Paul, I have to think that there is a reason God has allowed it to stay. I'm not saying I like it, or that God means to hurt me by not removing it, but what I have come to see, over time, is that not everything my anxiety has done to me is bad.

What if anxiety isn't just an enemy, but also, in ways that are too complicated to trace out fully, also an unexpected ally? Not just a closing off but an opening, a way for the Father himself to work, to pry apart our eyelids to things in life we might never have seen otherwise.

I remember the first time anxiety visited me, thinking that if I could just feel normal—even for a few hours—if I could just enjoy a cup of tea again, spontaneously laugh with a friend, leave the house without adrenaline pumping and throbbing through my veins, I'd be so grateful. I'd never take anything for granted again. Life, ordinary life, would be so beautiful.

Anxiety—indeed, suffering of any kind—allows us, if we let it, to open doors we might never have previously opened, doors of insight and sight, doors of empathy, doors to feel the Father's love and to love others in return. In going down to the pit, we have the opportunity to rise and to help others rise too. To be loved more deeply and to love more deeply. Perhaps, just perhaps, brokenness can lend us a greater wholeness of compassion in a way that holding it all together never could.

Through my journey with anxiety, too, I have grown in strength. But it is an upside-down strength, a paradoxical growth that I have found. It has come to me not so much through victories but in continual, cumulative meetings with weakness. Indeed, the more I see of this hard and beautiful world, and the more my heart is disillusioned, broken, stretched, the stronger I see him. 'For whenever I am weak, then I am strong' (2 Cor 12:10).

Anxiety teaches us, in the end, to abide in the one who welcomes our pain and who guarantees us he will never leave our side.

And to walk alongside others experiencing it, drawing from the depth of our own experience.

When I first 'got anxious', it was a foreign, strange experience. None of my friends had experienced it, not yet. I was the first, the trailblazer, out in the middle of the desert on my own, miles away from anyone I knew or anywhere I'd ever been. And yet since that time the distance has shrunk significantly. Over the years I've met friends, colleagues, fellow mums and, as I said in the beginning, even Uber drivers who've also met anxiety first-hand. While there's no secret handshake (especially not in 2020), there is a recognition, an ability to understand and comfort, that comes from personal experience. It seems I no longer stand in a desert but in a crowded room, where pain far more frequently overrides perfection as the dominant experience.

And in that crowded room, I begin to find my voice. And I hope that my words will in some way help others.

Anxiety then, as much as it has been my thorn, has also been my teacher. The cranky, crabby type who isn't known for smiling and whom you'd really rather not run into outside of school, if at all possible, but who still produces results. From my time in the valley with panic and trembling, where I still find myself at times, I have learnt truths both practical and spiritual. Therapists talk about acceptance and expansion as tools to dealing with anxiety. Accept the pain, stop fighting and fleeing, and also know that you are more than just it. Expand. And it will shrink. I like to think anxiety taught me to accept my humanity—to be humble and realistic in my humanness in this now-and-not-yet space—and to expand to see the Father's embodied compassion and divinity, not as something I need to stretch to touch, but as always wrapped around me, coming down to meet me. Anxiety has opened my faith-eyes to see him more clearly.

And as the years go on, I can see it more and more. Even something as hard-edged and prickly as anxiety can have its own beauty when brought into the light. But as my brother's poem 'atlas' said, it is an aching beauty that requires us to go down deep.

'Deep enough to understand that it's all too much to ever understand.'

And in the depths, beside us all along, is our elder brother Jesus.

Acknowledgements

To Gina: Story-shaper, wise-owl-eyed editor, serene-faced, big-hearted human being. Thanks for being the first to name the story. And for being my unflinching draft pen pal through the world's longest lockdown. Shalom.

To Lisa-Jo: Wordsmith, encourager, jacaranda-bright hope-holder. Thanks for helping me to see the 'life' in my writing and for teaching me how to take it out of the studio and into the company of others.

To Nate. It's been a joy to reconnect. I appreciate your lyrical words and generosity of spirit more than you can know. And to "the Fellas." Thanks for years of flower deliveries and thoughtful messages, and for being who you each are today in the world.

To Alix: When Gina sent out her networking lassos and looped our two lives together, I didn't know I'd find not only the fastest copyeditor on the east coast of Australia, but also a new friend. I look forward to more conversations about words that can be tidied and this messy life that can't always be. But for Grace.

To Inge: I love how you see the world and translate it so tangibly for others. Thanks for not only sharing your beautiful work so generously, but for being such a support through all of this. See you in NZ one day.

To James and Nicole at Ark House: Thanks for taking me on and for answering my countless emails. You make it all seem so breezy.

To the Wise Man and the Wise Woman: Your work is good and valuable and oh-so needed. Thankyou.

To my POP sisters: Here's to being partners in prayer for over two decades now. You girls are friendship gold. Bec, thanks for holding us all together with perseverance and joy even as we disperse throughout the world. Em and Kate, thanks for the early readings and enthusiastic feedback. And for so graciously being characters in the story. Your support in word and life means everything.

To Ronnie and Jane: I'm so glad we walked across the street from our apartment and into that school hall all those years ago. You know how much I admire (am in awe of) each of you. Women of talent, empathy and strength.

To Michael: Thanks for being our kids' Brisbane uncle, ever-patient removalist, puppy-sitter and fireside friend. Here's to more Beardys and piano in the future.

To my soul sisters, old and new: Beth, Sophia, Hayley, Shannon, Adela, Laurel, Jo, and Renee. Thanks for letting me be a small part of each of your tender and courageous stories.

FIGHT, FLIGHT AND FAITH

To Henri: For steadfastness and dangles, wherever the wind blows you.

To my new neighbour-sisters: Penny and Helen. I don't know what I did to deserve being planted in a corner of Queensland with you (nothing), but I'm sure glad I was. You guys are walking love in action.

To my over-the-sea family in Holland: Michelle, Herman, Jeanine, Emily, Bjorn, and Olaf, and Mark, Adele, Dave, and Lars. Our times together are not as often as we would like, but they are always so special.

To the Thompsons—Roz and Glenn, Briar, Chris and Lauren, Rich and Nic: I'm thankful to have been swallowed into the middle of such a big brood of fine individuals who make me laugh deep. Thanks for always having faith in my words, even when I haven't. If only we weren't separated by borders… but reunion will be extra sweet. Rich, thanks for being so generous with your gifts in launching this project.

And finally:

To Mum and Dad: I believe in superheros because I know you. Your support in this process has been nothing short of spectacular, as have your lives lived in such humility, generosity, and care. Suffering has not spared you, but you continue to pour out so much love. Thanks for trusting me with our story. Your hearts are living poetry. Greg would be so, so proud.

To Evangeline, Willem, and Joey: Gift-children. Confetti-covered surprises. Thanks for gratefully accepting cheese toasties and bowls of cereal and for putting up with having a writer for a mother. Let's keep making stories together. I love each of you more than you can ever know and can't wait to see what you create to make the world brighter and better.

To Mike: Thanks for being my best-friend-hug-husband-fellow-adventurer-gourmet-chef and always finest critic and first reader. Your epic faith in this story (and your willingness to let me tell it, knots and all) matches your commitment to our life through all seasons. It isn't always easy, but it is always good. From the moment I saw that backpack, I just knew we'd have tales to tell together. Let's celebrate and go on a writing retreat by the sea together…

And to Jesus: 'Let the words of my mouth and the meditation of my heart be acceptable to you, O LORD, my rock and my redeemer.' (Psalm 19:14)

About the author

NIKKI FLORENCE THOMPSON has a PhD in literature from Macquarie University and has taught undergraduate writing in Sydney, Brisbane, and Melbourne. She blogs at nikkifthompson.com on issues of faith, mental health, and parenting. Nikki loves living near the water in Queensland with her historian husband, Mike, three rambunctious children, and a highly photogenic puppy.

www.ingramcontent.com/pod-product-compliance
Lightning Source LLC
Chambersburg PA
CBHW071309110426
42743CB00042B/1230